Gingerbread Houses

a complete guide to baking, building, and decorating

Gingerbread Houses

a complete guide to baking, building, and decorating

CHRISTA CURRIE

ILLUSTRATED BY PATTI FALZARANO

BROADWAY BOOKS

NEW YORK

BROADWAY

A previous edition of this book was published in 1994 by Doubleday. It is here reprinted by arrangement with Doubleday.

Gingerbread Houses. Copyright © 1992, 1994 by Christa H. Currie. Illustrations Copyright © 1994 by Patti Falzarano. All rights reserved. Printed in the United States of America. No part of this book may be reproduced or transmitted in any form or by any means, electronic or mechanical, including photocopying, recopying, or by any information storage and retrieval system, without written permission from the publisher. For information, address: Broadway Books, a division of Random House, Inc., 1540 Broadway, New York, NY 10036.

Broadway Books titles may be purchased for business or promotional use or for special sales. For information, please write to: Special Markets Department, Random House, Inc., 1540 Broadway, New York, NY 10036.

BROADWAY BOOKS and its logo, a letter B bisected on the diagonal, are trademarks of Broadway Books, a division of Random House, Inc.

Visit our website at www.broadwaybooks.com

First Broadway Books trade paperback edition published 2001.

Book design by Gretchen Achilles

The Library of Congress has cataloged previous editions of this book as follows:

Currie, Christa.
Gingerbread houses: a complete guide to baking, building, and decorating / by Christa Currie.
p. cm.
1. Gingerbread. 2. Gingerbread houses. I. Title.
TT771.C87   1994   93-41695
   745.5—dc20   CIP

ISBN 0-385-47267-6

16   15   14   13   12   11   10   9   8

Contents

Gingerbread Houses

a complete guide to baking, building, and decorating

1.
Introduction

*W*hat do you need to make a gingerbread house? Essentially, an oven, a good recipe, some time, and a little imagination. A buddy is not a bad idea either—a spouse, pal, parent, or child. Gingerbreading is fun for all ages.

The purpose of this book is first to reassure you that you *can* indeed make a house like the one illustrated in Figure 1.

Fig. 1
(opposite)

Every time I go into a craft shop or attend a bazaar or fair, I look enviously at all the handmade items, think how I could make them (and not have to pay *that* price), go home, and promptly postpone making the item until making it no longer seems important. Why do I procrastinate? Well, usually, because I need some reassurance that my project will turn out and not be a waste of time and money and that I will be proud of what I've accomplished. I need instructions that will make me believe I will have success, instructions that are easy to read, answer my most basic questions, and leave me feeling that I can do that. Naturally, the simpler the instructions are to understand, the more likely I am to attempt to follow them.

The instructions that follow are simple yet detailed enough to take anyone through to a successful product—a darling gingerbread house.

Several years ago I was reading through a national ladies' magazine and saw an invitation to participate in a gingerbread house contest. I'd never made a gingerbread house and didn't even know anyone who had, but I decided that I wanted to enter that contest. It was definitely a case of "I can do that!" The magazine provided the basic instructions. All I had to provide was the original design, the elbow grease, and a great deal of innovation. I learned a lot in the process, and I won fifth place honorable mention with my very first house! Granted, not first, not second place—no, fifth place honorable mention. But—*nationwide!* My first house! Not only was I proud, I was hooked on gingerbreading.

Which leads me to the second reason for this book.

That first year I learned many things the magazine didn't tell me about making gingerbread houses. And after ten years of making gingerbread houses for fun and profit, I've amassed a mountain more of knowledge. In this book I share some of the many things I've learned—such as how to perk up a house you made a year or two ago; how to make your chimney smoke; how to light your house; how to store your house; and so on. I found that although you can bake a house in the round, it's not too practical and it's very tricky—thus only for advanced gingerbreaders. Through trial and error, I also discovered that if I designed a house that was significantly taller than its base was wide (got that?), without additional support it would most likely fall over.

I also found I could make houses in July and use them as gifts in December. Better yet, I found I could make houses in July and *sell* them in December. Even better, I found I could teach others how to make houses and earn money without having to clean up *my* kitchen.

A gingerbread house can be as complicated as you want to make it. If you've looked at magazine features on gingerbread houses, you know that a replica of the White House or the Taj Mahal is not unattainable. In fact, such a creation can be a delightful challenge, one the true artiste in all of us may wish at one time or another to tackle. But . . .

First and foremost, gingerbreading should be fun, a family affair. A beautiful, basic house that delights young and old alike is the type of house I'm dedicated to helping you make here—not a White House replica or the Taj Mahal. I'll give you hints to start you on your way to Washington, D.C., or India if you've got that bug, but just hints. This book is only for fun! And a little profit, if you're so inclined.

There isn't a child alive who isn't mesmerized by a gingerbread house. In fact, most adults become children when they see one. It doesn't matter if your house is decorated perfectly or not. A three-year-old can stick candy on a house and it will look absolutely charming when you sparkle the house with edible glitter and add a lollipop tree or two. It doesn't matter if that large gumdrop is stuck on the side of the house or the top. There is no one way to decorate a house. And if you happen to go way into left field while gingerbreading, one of the nicest things is there's no waste. You can eat your leftovers or even your mistakes.

Thus, here are the most important rules of gingerbreading:

1. There is no right or wrong way to decorate a ginger-
    bread house—there is only the fun way.

2. There is no age requirement for decorating a ginger-
    bread house. If you're old enough to restrain yourself
    from immediately eating every piece of candy in sight,
    you're old enough to decorate a gingerbread house.

4

2.
Steps to Gingerbreading

*L*et's get down to making your first gingerbread house. Basically, there are three steps to this process. You will have to:

1. Transfer the pattern (see "Tracing the Pattern" on pages 10–12) and follow it to cut out your gingerbread house pieces.

2. Cut out (see "Cutting Out Your House" on pages 27–28), then bake and trim (see "Trimming Baked Dough" on pages 28–29) your gingerbread house.

3. Assemble (see Chapter 6) and decorate (see Chapter 7) your gingerbread house.

We will go through each step in detail, so that you're very comfortable with the process. *I suggest that you scan through the whole book before starting on your house.* At the very least, look over the "Checklist for Building Your First House" at the end of the book. It will give you a good idea of what you need in order to create a bit of magic.

Time Requirements

Depending on the type of house you make and how elaborately you decorate it, figure about one and a half hours for baking the house; another half hour to forty-five minutes for assembling the house; and anywhere from ten minutes (if you're three years old) to four hours for decorating; four to six hours drying time before spraying it with a protective sealant. (See "Acrylic Sealer" on pages 92–94.)

"Four *hours* to decorate!" you exclaim.

Well, I've spent literally days on a three-story, hillside, custom-made English Tudor house. It's hard to say when you're done with a house—mainly because the decorating possibilities are endless, and my philosophy is that a gingerbread house *cannot* be overdecorated. They are supposed to be *busy*! All in all, though, you should figure that you're going to invest about six or so hours from start to finish in your first house. But you're going to like doing it—especially the decorating part.

3.
Patterns

Basic House

Figures 2 and 3 show the pattern for a basic house. Its finished size is 6.75 by 8 inches at the base, and it stands about 8.75 inches high without the chimney. This is a very good size for a gingerbread house because it's easy to work with as well to landscape (with trees, fences, and the like). After you're finished decorating, all the yardwork makes the house look much larger. And advanced gingerbreaders will find that adding a balcony or a porch or even a dormer to this basic house changes its appearance so dramatically that this might be the one pattern they'll turn to on a regular basis over the years. I've done other patterns, but for overall look and ease in assembling, this is my favorite style.

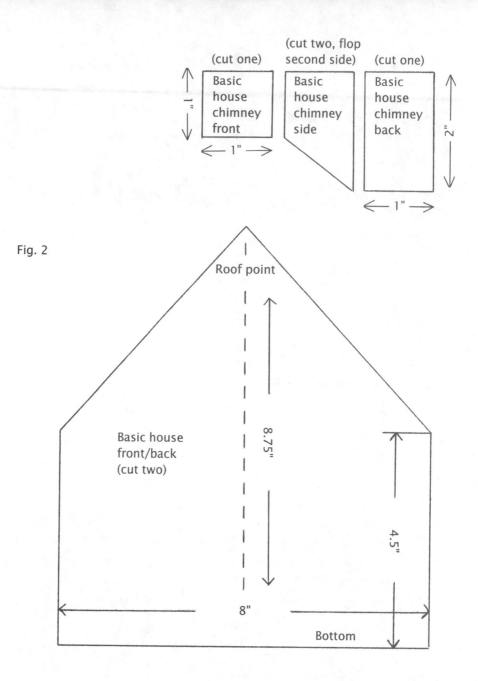

(cut one)
Basic house chimney front

1"

← 1" →

(cut two, flop second side)
Basic house chimney side

(cut one)
Basic house chimney back

2"

← 1" →

Fig. 2

Roof point

Basic house front/back
(cut two)

8.75"

4.5"

8"

Bottom

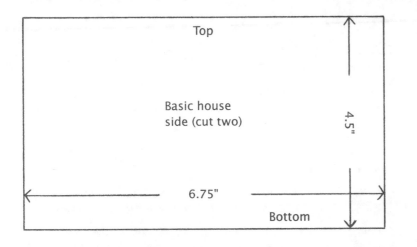

Top

Basic house
side (cut two)

4.5"

6.75"

Bottom

Fig. 3

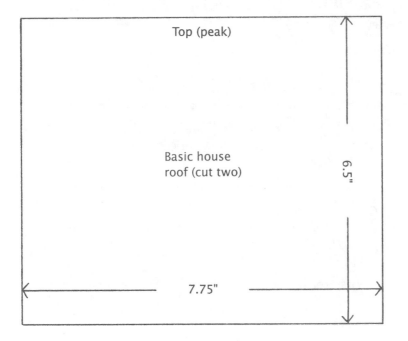

Top (peak)

Basic house
roof (cut two)

6.5"

7.75"

TRACING THE PATTERN

Draw the basic house pattern from Figures 2 and 3 onto an old file folder, stenciling paper, or acetate sheets. The next two sections describe the benefits of each material.

One-Time-Use Pattern If you're in a big hurry and don't want to plan ahead for future building projects (this is the way I usually work), find a couple of pieces of thin cardboard 8.5 inches by 11 inches to trace the basic pattern onto. An old file folder works great. I've routinely recycled the front and back covers of my telephone directories for this purpose. Don't use paper lighter in weight, because a pattern has to take a lot of abuse. If you're careful when cutting out the gingerbread pieces, you'll be able to use a file-folder pattern several times.

Fig. 4 (opposite)

Multiple-Use Pattern If you're past the immediate-gratification stage and have decided that you really want your patterns to have a long and useful life, you should purchase stenciling paper or heavier weight mylar plastic stencil sheets (sometimes called acetate sheets). Neither is cheap, especially when compared to the cost of your telephone directory covers, but the cost is not totally outrageous and patterns made from them will last practically forever—in fact, the plastic stencil patterns will become family heirlooms. A local printer or crafters' supply store should carry these products.

Whatever material you decide to use, place a piece of carbon paper between the full-sized pattern and it. Then, using a

pencil and a straightedge, trace the pieces onto the transfer material. Finally, cut out the pattern.

LABELING PATTERN PIECES

After you've cut out your pattern pieces, label each piece with its name (roof, front/back, side), a name that you've chosen for your house ("basic" is a good name for this one), and the number of pieces of gingerbread you'll need to cut for from each pattern piece (as I've labeled the pieces in this book).

Store your patterns in individual large, zip-lock type bags, along with any hints you may have discovered while working on a particular house. Enclosing a photo of the finished house is also a great idea so you can repeat your decorating success. (These photos also form the basis for your portfolio if you decide to sell your houses.)

Design Your Own

To make your own gingerbread house pattern, I strongly recommend you use graph paper because the little blue squares ensure that right angles really are right angles. Because each square can represent 1 inch, matching the sides and roof is much easier.

No matter what type of house you want to build, your standard house pattern will consist of three pieces: (1) side, (2) front/back, and (3) roof. Additional pieces, such as chimneys, dormers, porches/balconies, and the like, are accessories to the standard house pattern. Some of the more common ac-cessories are discussed in detail in Chapter 7.

BASE HOUSE

The key to designing your own pattern is making sure that the connecting sides of the house are all exactly the same height. (See Figure 5.) If they aren't, your roof will fall off. How's that for incentive to measure carefully? This is where those little blue squares come in mighty handy. If your house front pattern is 4.5 squares high, your house side *must* be 4.5 squares high.

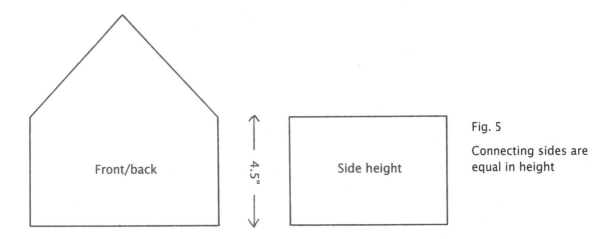

Front/back

4.5"

Side height

Fig. 5

Connecting sides are equal in height

ROOF

The roof is a bit trickier (for me to explain, not for you to do). Each piece will be a large rectangle. First, measure the width of the house side pattern piece. (See Figure 6.) Add 1 inch to that measurement. For instance, if your house side measures 6.75

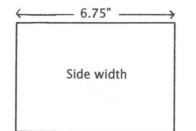

6.75"

Side width

Fig. 6

The width of the roof is 7.75 inches

Fig. 7

The depth of the roof is 6.5 inches

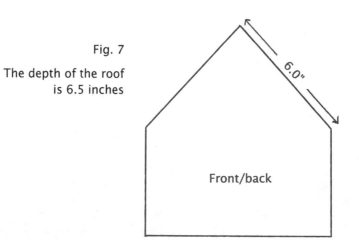

6.0"

Front/back

GINGERBREAD HOUSES

inches from front to back, the width of your roof rectangle will be 7.75 inches.

The second measurement you need for your roof is the distance from the peak of the front/back house piece to the end of the slant, plus .5 inch. (See Figure 7.) For instance, if that

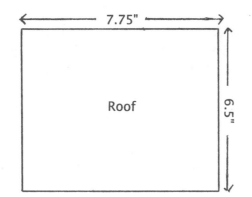

7.75"

Roof

6.5"

Fig. 8

7.75 inches (Fig. 6) by 6.5 inches (Fig. 7) = roof size

slanted edge measures 6 inches, the depth of your roof rectangle would be 6.5 inches. Why do you need the "extra" inches? They make the overhang and eaves on your house. If you want more overhang, increase the roof size accordingly.

In this example, your finished roof pattern would be a rectangle that is 7.75 inches by 6.5 inches in size. (See Figure 8.)

As you become more proficient at making patterns, you'll find that your gingerbread houses can have walls that slant inward or outward, roofs that are trapezoidal, and chimneys that are just plain lopsided. Your imagination can take wing and the style possibilities become endless.

Copying a Real House

I don't recommend that novice gingerbread house builders attempt to copy a real house. Doing so requires some careful computation and experience in pattern design. However, if you're quite confident and determined, here are the guidelines to help you copy a real house into gingerbread.

The most important part of making a replica in gingerbread is getting the dimensions of the real house correct. To do this, you can take actual measurements of the house (for instance, house sides are 28 feet across and 16 feet high). Translate these measurements into inches (house sides are 28 *inches* across and 16 *inches* high). Divide these measurements by 4* (house sides equal 28 inches divided by 4, or 7 inches across, and 16 inches divided by 4, or 4 inches high.) Thus, the pattern piece for the house side should be 7 inches across and 4 inches high.

If the house has many nooks and juts and you want them in your gingerbread likeness, you have to measure each one as well as the distance each is from either end of the house. Obviously, this can be a formidable task if the house is very large and has a complex design. However, when you successfully replicate an intricate design, you'll feel a tremendous amount of pride.

*Note: Dividing by 4 is discretionary. If you want your house smaller or larger, find a common denominator that will result in a house of the desired size. For example, if you want a large replica of the sample house used above, divide by 1, thus creating a gingerbread house that is 28 inches wide and 16 inches tall. For a much smaller model, divide by 7. The resulting house will then be 4 inches wide and 2.3 inches high.

Of course, if you're unable to go and measure the White House personally, you'll need some good photos and the ability to figure the size ratios among building components.

I guess the natural question here is: Why would anyone want to reproduce a real house in gingerbread?

Well, a real estate friend of mine made a replica of each house she sold and presented it to her buyers at Christmas. Needless to say, she never had to hunt for clients. I think they moved every several years just to get a new gingerbread house.

I've given "replica" gingerbread houses as housewarming gifts to good friends. The houses will last several years if they're treated gently, so giving someone a gingerbread house in July, or January, or October, or anytime is never inappropriate. And you can bet the gesture will be remembered!

4.
Supplies and Equipment Needed

Base for House

The base (or yard) of your gingerbread house can be anything you want it to be: a wooden board covered with foil, an old serving tray, essentially anything flat and somewhat sturdy. You will want this base to be about 4 inches larger all around than the base dimensions of your house so you will have room to landscape. The pattern in this book will result in a house that has an area of 8 by 6.75 inches, so you will want a baseboard with an approximate surface of 12 by 11 inches.

Before you choose what to use as a base, decide now if you will want to light your house. See pages 95–97 for details of lighting.

As a base, I highly recommend 1-inch-thick Styrofoam. (Any thinner and it won't be strong enough to hold your house. Any thicker, however, is just a waste of money.) In fact, unless you use Styrofoam as a base, you may have to forgo any large posted objects, such as peppermint candy stick trees, or very tall heavy objects. And if you use a Styrofoam base, lighting your house will be much easier. (See Chapter 7.)

Hold on now—I am very appreciative of the "eco-horrid" attitude on Styrofoam, but there is *good* Styrofoam (crunchy stuff) and *bad* Styrofoam (made with little beadlike material). The state of Oregon (where I'm from) has banned bad Styrofoam—the kind that spews fluorocarbons into the atmosphere and attacks the ozone layer. The good Styrofoam, however, can be purchased at any craft store, in any size and in any shape. You can buy a round piece, a square piece, an oblong piece—or you can cut it easily into the shape you prefer. I, for example, cut out large stars for children to assemble small houses on.

Regardless of what type of base you decide to use, consider covering its bottom with some sort of soft material so it won't scratch the surface it will ultimately sit on. Gingerbread houses, when completed, are heavy and pushing them around can cause scratches. I use felt, but any fabric glued to the underside of the baseboard will do nicely.

You might also want to consider putting feet on your base, especially if you're using Styrofoam. You can cut the feet out of extra pieces of Styrofoam. Feet raise the board from the table surface, making the gingerbread house easier to lift. (See Figure 9.)

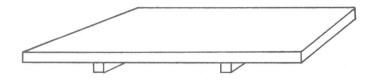

Fig. 9

Base board with feet

Baking Supplies

To bake your house, you will need a few basic items most of us already have in our kitchens. Obviously, you will need an oven. Unless you're camping in the Rockies, that's probably a given. To round out this list, you'll also need:

- *2 large cookie sheets* Totally flat sheets are the easiest to work with, but they are expensive; if you don't already have them, don't go out and buy them just for this. If you use jelly roll pans, which have a lip all around them, you must fill the pan with ¼-inch-thick piece of plywood. You will be rolling your gingerbread dough on the back of the pan and will need the wood to fit into the pan to brace it. (See Figure 10.) Without this brace, the pan will cave in or at least bend, which will also bend your gingerbread pieces.

- *A dish towel*

- *A rolling pin*

SUPPLIES AND EQUIPMENT NEEDED

- *A sharp, straight-edge knife or X-acto knife*

- *House pattern* See Chapter 3 to prepare your pattern for cutting.

- *Small cookie cutters* (For cut-out windows—about 1 to 1½ inches in diameter in various shapes—hearts, circles, diamonds, and so on)

- *Gingerbread dough*

Fig. 10

Brace under cookie sheet

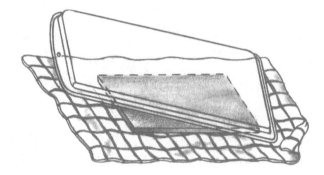

Decorating Supplies

You will need the following items to decorate your gingerbread house. I'll explain how you use each one in Chapter 7.

- *Frosting decorating bags* At least one, fairly large bag to start with. Buy more as you become more comfortable with decorating and want to add different color frostings to your house. Use commercial cloth bags, disposable, reusable or plastic ones, or ones you make from parchment.

- *6 standard size couplers* One set for each bag you use is sufficient, but they're like hairpins—they seem to disappear on their own—so get extras.

- *4 metal decorating tips* Nos. 3 (small dot); 12 (large dot); 16 (small star); 21 (large star). Also buy a tip-cleaning brush.

- *Candies* See Chapter 7.

Generally, instructions for assembling the bags with their tips and couplers are given on the box in which they are sold, so I won't go into that here. Any store that sells cake decorating supplies and/or crafts will have decorating bags as well as couplers and tips and will be able to show you how to assemble and use them.

The decorating tips I recommend here will get you started and are sufficient for decorating a house very nicely. Later, as your decorating becomes more elaborate, I suggest you buy two or three of each tip so you can change tips and colors without having to wash everything each time you change. By that time, too, you'll probably recognize the potential of other style tips and will want to add those as well. Wilton (a national manufacturer of cake decorating supplies) makes decorating bags, tips, and couplers, and provides suggestions for their use. Please refer to their in-store displays for further information.

5.
Recipes, Cutting, and Baking

*P*lease read this whole section before starting. Or review page 113, "Before You Begin, Decide." By the time you've done everything in this chapter, your house will be ready to assemble and decorate.

Making the Gingerbread

The following gingerbread recipe is the one I use for my houses, the one with which I've had the most success. You can vary the spices according to your taste and the ultimate use you plan for your gingerbread. I generally don't eat my houses, so I don't use ginger and nutmeg because they are expensive. But adding both to this recipe changes it from just the acceptable-tasting cookie you get using cinnamon to very tasty gingerbread. If you want to use the other spices, I have indicated the amounts to substitute for the cinnamon.

I don't recommend any recipe requiring eggs. I find eggs make a "cakey" cookie that does not hold up well if you're using it for construction purposes. You can refrigerate the dough for a couple of weeks or freeze it for several months. Return refrigerated dough to room temperature and defrost frozen dough overnight in the refrigerator. Then reknead the dough until it is smooth and even colored. Next roll it out and proceed as usual.*

GINGERBREAD

Preheat the oven to 375° F.
In a large pot on low heat, melt

1 CUP VEGETABLE SHORTENING

1 CUP GRANULATED SUGAR

1 CUP DARK MOLASSES

Remove from heat and mix in

1 TEASPOON BAKING SODA

½ TEASPOON SALT

1 TABLESPOON GROUND CINNAMON†

Stir in thoroughly 1 cup at a time

4½ TO 5 CUPS SIFTED ALL-PURPOSE FLOUR

* If your dough is very cold or is being reused from a previous rolling, warm it in a microwave for 10 to 15 seconds and then reknead it. But watch the time carefully: The dough may get very hot, and you don't want to cook it.

†If desired, substitute: 3 teaspoons ground ginger and 1 teaspoon ground nutmeg for the cinnamon.

Mix and knead all the ingredients until the dough is even in color and smooth, not crumbly or dry. Form the dough into a log, and divide the log into three pieces. Wrap two pieces in plastic wrap to keep them from drying out while you are working with the other piece.

Cutting Out Your House

1. Place your cookie sheet facedown on a damp kitchen towel. (This will keep it from sliding around.)

2. Roll the unwrapped dough out on the back of cookie sheet, covering the entire cookie sheet with dough. (Use your wood brace if you use jelly roll pans; see page 21.) Roll the dough out to about ⅛- to ⅜-inch thick. Take your time! This dough is heavy and requires a light touch so it won't stick to your rolling pin or break up. Do not use too much flour on your rolling pin while rolling—just enough to keep the dough from sticking. The dough gets easier to handle as it gets thinner. Keep in mind that any patching you do will show on your baked house, so work carefully.

3. Lay your first pattern piece lightly on the rolled-out dough. With planning, you can get several pattern pieces (perhaps one roof piece and the two side pieces) on one sheet. (See Figure 11.) Leave at least ½ inch between pieces to allow for cookie spread while baking.

4. Cut around the pattern with a knife or X-acto knife.

5. After cutting several pattern pieces, lift the dough scraps off the cookie sheet and wrap them in plastic wrap for another rolling.

Fig. 11

Pattern pieces on dough

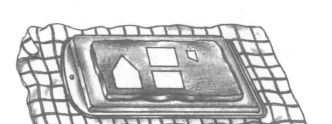

If you're going to cut out the windows and doors on your house, do it now. After determining where you'll want to place them and what shape you prefer them to be, take your cookie cutter (or knife) and cut out the pieces. Remove the cut-out window or door and use it for subsequent rollings. If you just want an outline of a window or door for decorating purposes, leave the cut-out in the house piece while baking. If you leave the cut-out in the house piece by mistake while it bakes, you can remove it after it is baked if you work very fast while the cookie is still hot and soft.

6. Now bake your cut-out pieces at 375° F. for 10 to 14 minutes (depending on your oven), until it is a nice reddish brown color. You should be able to touch the cookie and not leave an imprint. If you do leave an imprint, bake it for another 3 to 4 minutes.

7. Your cookie is going to spread while it bakes. Therefore:

Trimming Baked Dough

Leave the cookies on the baking sheet, lay your pattern piece back over the baked cookie, and cut around the pattern with a knife to trim off the excess. (Use an oven mitt to hold the pattern on the hot cookie. If you have long nails, they work well also.) The cookie is very easy to cut while it is hot. Once it cools (in 1½ to 2 minutes), it is too crisp to trim safely. You can make minor adjustments at assembly time—we'll go over how to do it then. If you must, you can pop the pieces back in the oven for a moment to soften them up for additional trimming, but you'll have to work fast.

When the trimmed cookies are fairly cool and will hold their shape, remove them from the cookie sheet, supporting them carefully. Let them thoroughly cool on a rack. Once the cookies are cooled, you can place them on any flat surface until you are ready to assemble and decorate the house.

Decorating Icing

Decorating icing is an icing that dries to a hard, candylike finish. Whatever you make with it will last a long time. It is not used to frost cakes, but only to make long-lasting decorations. It is completely edible and can be tinted with food coloring. It is ideal for your gingerbread house; not only will your decorations last a long time, but decorating icing is the cement that will hold your house together.

There are various recipes for decorating icing. I will provide you with two versions—one using meringue powder and one using fresh egg whites.

I recommend using meringue powder rather than egg whites to make decorating icing. The egg white icing, though less expensive to make, can be used to hold your house to-

Be sure to keep your baked cookies away from any high moisture–producing source, such as a boiling teapot or a dishwasher in midcycle. The cookies will absorb any moisture in the air readily.

Whether you are working with egg whites or meringue powder, make sure that all your utensils are grease-free. Any oil or grease will break down the mixture and you'll have egg white or meringue powder soup. (Not bad for the dog's cholesterol count, but awful for gingerbread houses.)

Keep unused portions of your decorating icing covered. It dries out very quickly, and if you're not careful you'll have a cement-hard lump in the bottom of your mixing bowl.

gether only right at the time it is made. While you can use it later on for decorating, it is never again strong enough to use as mortar. Plus, in some areas of the country, people have been warned not to eat raw eggs. Icing made from meringue powder is safer to use than that made from raw egg whites. Also, when I'm on a house-making binge (you'll go on one too, because once people see your house, they'll all want one), I have a very difficult time getting rid of all those yolks—the family's sick of yellow cake and the dog's cholesterol is out of sight, and I can't justify just throwing them away. There—you have my reasons for using meringue powder icing. Now you have to make up your own mind.

Most grocery stores carry meringue powder. It is usually found in the cake aisle. A four-ounce container of meringue powder will make five or six batches of icing; and you'll need approximately two batches per house.

A piece of plastic wrap pushed around the icing (no air bubbles) will protect it while you are decorating. To store the icing overnight or longer, you must use plastic wrap *and* foil or a sealed container. Refrigerate the icing if you are storing it overnight.

You must rebeat both the meringue powder icing and the egg white icing before you use them if you have left them for a day or more. The rebeaten meringue powder icing will work very well to glue another house together; as mentioned, the egg white icing will not keep its cementing properties after the initial beating.

You will need to make two batches of whichever icing you decide to use. Unless you have a heavy-duty mixer, I suggest you fix each batch separately.

MERINGUE POWDER ICING
(1 BATCH)

Empty into large mixing bowl

4 CUPS (1 POUND) POWDERED SUGAR

3 TABLESPOONS MERINGUE POWDER

Add

6 TO 8 TABLESPOONS WARM WATER

With an electric mixer, blend the ingredients on low speed, then beat on high speed for 6 to 8 minutes, or until the mixture holds a stiff peak. If the icing is too thick, add a little more water (1 *teaspoon* at a time). You will want it to hold a peak but not be so stiff that you can't push it through a decorating tip. Trial and error are the best teachers here.

EGG WHITE ICING
(1 BATCH)

Empty into large mixing bowl

4 CUPS (1 POUND) POWDERED SUGAR

Add

2 LARGE EGG WHITES
½ TEASPOON CREAM OF TARTAR
3 TO 4 TEASPOONS WARM WATER

With an electric mixer, blend the ingredients on low speed, then beat on high speed for 8 to 10 minutes, or until the mixture holds a stiff peak. If icing is too thick, add a little more water (¼ *teaspoon* at a time). You want it to hold a peak but not be so stiff you can't push it through a decorating tip. Trial and error are the best teachers here.

COLORING THE ICING

If I'm going to decorate with color, I usually make a double batch of decorating icing and tint ½ to ¾ cup in the colors of my choice. Most of my icing I keep white, though—it looks great with any candy and makes super snow for your house. (See "Icicles" and "Snow" on pages 88 and 89.)

To color icing, food coloring paste works much better than food coloring drops. Coloring paste is a commercially prepared food dye that comes in a multitude of colors (including black)

and is very thick, thus allowing you to achieve a lot of color without changing the texture of the icing. The drops add too much liquid and the icing could get runny before you get the shade you want. Also, pastes are more intense in color and work better for those Christmas reds and greens. However, if you are working in pastels and your icing is a tad too stiff to work with, food coloring drops will work wonders.

Icing colored with paste food coloring intensifies as it dries. So what may look like a light red will probably dry to a deep red. Keep this in mind when you are adding color.

Where do you get paste food coloring? It's available in any store that sells cake decorating supplies. While the paste is usually sold individually and may seem expensive, a little jar goes a long way.

6.
Assembling Your House

To assemble the house, you're going to need your cookie pieces, a base-board (we'll discuss this further shortly), and a pastry bag fitted with a #12 (large dot) tip and filled with white decorating icing.

I usually bake, assemble, and decorate my houses in one session—making an entire day of it. If you prefer, you can bake and assemble on one day, then decorate on the next. But be careful about letting your baked pieces sit around. As I've mentioned, gingerbread collects moisture. If you live in a humid climate, your house pieces could become soft and impossible to build with. By baking and assembling in one day, the mortar frosting helps stabilize the house so it won't absorb moisture so readily. You can then decorate your house at a more leisurely pace.

Should assembly be unavoidably delayed, you can stick your house pieces in the oven for a few additional minutes to dry them out again—just be *very* careful they don't burn, and keep them flat. Also, check if they need to be trimmed again.

*Bracing the House**

If you're concerned about humid weather or about the height of your house (the sides of a tall house can buckle or collapse completely under the weight of a roof), you can brace the sides with craft (Popsicle) sticks. (Craft stores sell them by the box.) After you've cut out and baked the pieces, glue the sticks to their insides using decorating icing as glue or with a glue gun. I don't recommend using hot syrup as an adhesive here. It sets up too quickly and is difficult to handle on large surfaces. (See pages 37–46 for the pros and cons of these three methods.) Make sure the sticks don't extend beyond the edge of the gingerbread. (Ideally, try to leave about ⅛-inch margin.) Otherwise you won't be able to line up adjoining pieces when assembling your house.

If the house you are making is very large or stands very tall, take a thin (⅛-inch) sheet of Styrofoam and cut out an exact replica of the pattern pieces. Trim the Styrofoam pieces so they are approximately an ⅛ inch smaller all around than the cookies; then glue them to the back sides of the cut-out cookie pieces. Again, you can use the decorating icing as glue or use a glue gun. This sort of brace is very strong.

---

* Houses made from the pattern in this book usually don't require any bracing.

GINGERBREAD HOUSES

Assembling with Icing

1. Have ready a couple of spice jars or small cans to brace the first piece of your house.

2. Fit a decorating bag with the #12 (large dot) tip and fill the bag three-quarters full with the white decorating icing. I will be using the word "generous" throughout these instructions to describe icing strips. By generous, I mean a strip approximately ⅜ inch wide and as deep. The icing is all that keeps your house together, so don't skimp here. The icing here will show on your finished product, so try to apply it evenly.

3. Envision how your house is going to sit on the baseboard. Using the front/back pattern piece as a guide, mark with a pencil where the front of the house will sit. (See Figure 12.) Don't worry about the pencil mark, it will be snowed over.

NOTE:

If you're going to light your house, read the "Lighting" section on pages 95–97 before doing anything else.

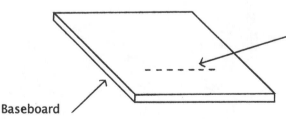

Approximate location of house front

Baseboard

Fig. 12

4. Test to make sure your cookie pieces fit together snugly before you cement your house. A bump on the side of the cookie will result in a gaping hole or a lopsided door or chimney. If you need to correct a piece (straighten out the roof or side of a door, a shutter, a chimney piece, for example), very, very carefully shave the cookie edge using a serrated knife. Filing the cookie edge with an emery board is even better. Work slowly so you don't break the cookie. Also, make sure your icing is well away from the sawdust. Though you can make these minor adjustments after you've decorated the cookie, there's less chance of spoiling your decorations if you shave or file before you decorate.

5. Hold the front piece of your house and squeeze icing generously along the bottom edge. Place this section

Fig. 13

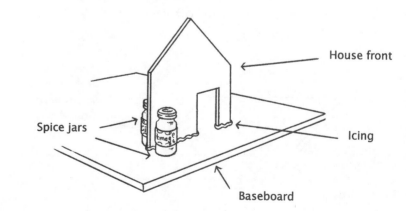

House front

Spice jars

Icing

Baseboard

GINGERBREAD HOUSES

over the penciled guide on the baseboard and prop it up with a spice jar on either side. (See Figure 13.) Within a few minutes, the icing will have hardened and you can remove the props.

6. Squeeze icing generously along the bottom edge of a house side piece. Also squeeze icing along one front edge of this cookie. With a gentle pressure, attach the house side to the front at a right angle, making sure the two pieces are as tight as possible against one another where they meet. There's no need to prop the side up with jars; it will stay upright by itself now.

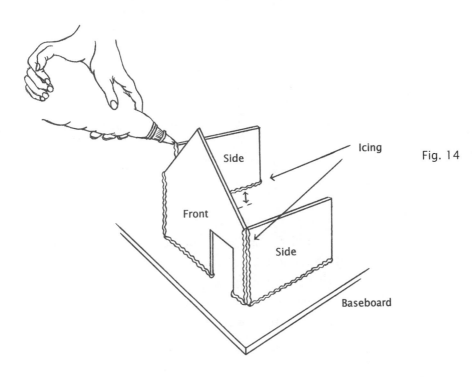

Fig. 14

39

7. Attach the second side of the house to the front piece in the same manner as in step 6. (See Figure 14.)

8. Squeeze icing generously on the bottom edge and the two side edges of the back piece of your house. Align this cookie with the already attached side pieces. (See Figure 15.)

Fig. 15

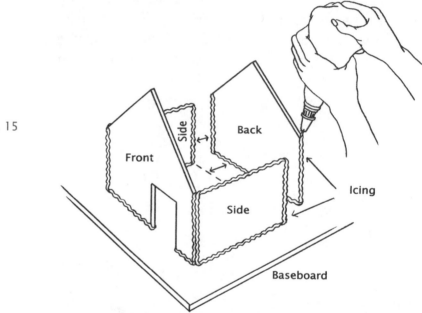

Side

Back

Front

Side

Icing

Baseboard

9. Congratulations! You should now have a house—roofless, but freestanding (no more spice jars). However, for that extra bit of insurance, squeeze a strip of icing along the *inside* bottom edges where they meet the base and into each inside corner of your house.

10. To attach the roof, squeeze a generous amount of icing along one slanted upper edge of both of the front and the back pieces (work with one side of the roof at a time) and across the top of the adjoining side piece. Place the roof piece carefully on the slants so that the roof's peak is even with the points of the front and back sides. (See Figure 16.) You should have about a half inch of eaves hanging over the side of your house.

NOTE:

If you've cut out your windows and want to decorate the *inside* of your house, do that now. You may also want to decorate the windows now—some people find it easier to do before they put the roof on.

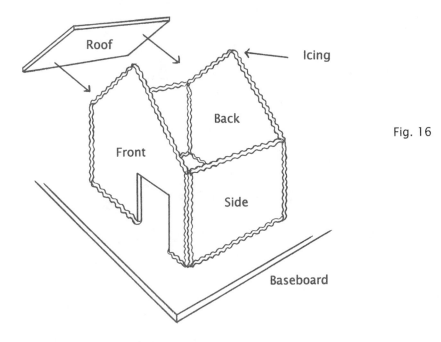

Fig. 16

11. Squeeze a generous amount of icing along the other slants of the two front and back pieces, across the top of the roof piece already in place, and across the top of

the remaining side piece. Lay your second roof piece along the slants, making sure it fits snugly against the peak of the first roof piece. (See Figure 17.) Again you should have about a half inch of eaves hanging over the side of your house.

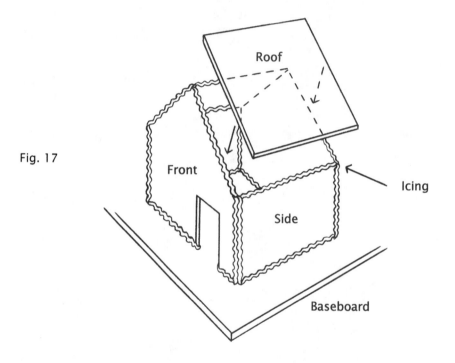

Fig. 17

Roof

Front

Side

Icing

Baseboard

12. If you're adding a chimney (see pages 64–65), you can do so now, or you can wait until you decorate your roof to add it.

GINGERBREAD HOUSES

You can place the chimney anywhere on the roof (across the peak or right in the middle of a roof side). Using the chimney gingerbread pieces included with this book and decorator icing or a glue gun, you're going to assemble the chimney by making a small box.

a. Working with the *first side piece*, pipe icing along the slanted edge of the chimney side. Place this piece (point side down) at a right angle to one side of the roof. The top of the chimney piece can fall anywhere on the roof, but for this illustration have the top of the slant just meet the peak on the roof. The squared part of the piece will stick up above the roof peak. Hold the piece in place until it stays by itself.

b. Then, using the *back piece*, pipe icing along one long side and on the bottom. Attach the long side of the back piece at a right angle to the long side of the se-cured side piece attached in step a, making sure the tops of the two pieces are even. You may have to pipe additional icing along the bottom of the back piece to make sure it's securely attached to the roof.

c. Now, using the *second side piece*, pipe icing along the long side and slanted side. Position this piece (point side down) along the remaining long side of the chim-ney back and onto the roof slant. Again, make sure the tops of all three pieces are level.

d. Finally, take up the small, square *front piece*. Pipe icing along the bottom and two sides of this piece. Position this piece (uniced side up) onto the roof peak while gently pushing it onto the extended side pieces of the chimney. (See Figure 18.)

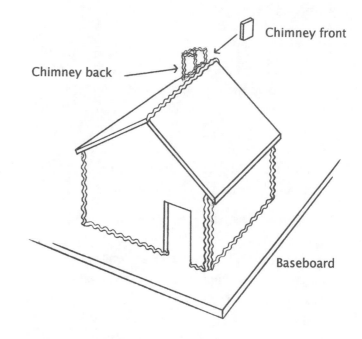

Fig. 18

Chimney assembly

Chimney front

Chimney back

Baseboard

Looking down onto your roof, the chimney should look like an open-topped box. If it's a little crooked, that's okay, it only adds to the charm of the house.

Now you're ready to decorate.

Assembling with a Glue Gun

Another way to assemble your gingerbread house is to follow all of the preceding assembly instructions but use glue from a glue gun as the adhesive. Of course, you would use glue only on an *inedible* house. The only cautions about using a glue gun are: (1) They get very hot and could seriously burn young children, and (2) the glue will melt Styrofoam and, thus, the baseboard, if you are using that type of base. To help avoid this problem, hold the gun a bit away from the intended glue area—this will allow the glue to cool a little before it hits the Styrofoam. It's tricky—too close and the glue is too hot; too far away and the glue dries before it is used. Experiment. Keep in mind that gunned glue can always be reinforced with decorating icing.

You might be wondering why you would want to glue your house together.

The main advantage is that if you're planning to keep your house year after year, the glue assembly method seems to last longer than the icing method. The major problem I find with keeping a house for a long time is that the gingerbread cookie has a tendency to absorb moisture not only from the air, but also from the icing that holds the house together. Over time, the icing becomes so dry that it crumbles and your walls come tumbling down. Using glue helps avoid this.

Assembling with Hot Syrup

Houses also can be cemented together with a hot syrup, instead of either icing or glue. The biggest problems I have with the syrup method is: (1) It's another cooking project (I like to decorate, not cook), and (2) the syrup is very hot and shouldn't be used around children. However, if you want to use syrup to assemble your house, use a good hard candy recipe. After the candy has come to the hard ball stage but is still liquid, dip your cookie pieces into it (or drizzle the syrup onto the cookie) and then, working very quickly, place the cookie in its appropriate spot.

Syrup, when cooled, forms an extremely strong mortar for your house and is edible too—sort of the best of two worlds: tasty and strong. But the syrup method is for experienced gingerbreaders only. Once you've attached one cookie to another with hot syrup, it's there to stay—crooked or not. Additionally, I don't recommend that you use hot syrup for anything except assembling the house. Using it to attach small items (candies, cookies, braces) is rather risky as the liquid syrup is extremely hot and you could easily burn yourself. Use the decorating icing instead.

7.
Decorating Your House

*B*efore you pick up your decorating tubes, determine what you're going to do first. (See "Before You Begin, Decide" on page 113.)

Plan to decorate from the inside out. Specifically, if you decide to decorate the inside of your house, do it before you start doing the outside. Of course, for interior decorating the roof has to be off the house so you can gain access. Suggestions for decorating the inside include placing a sugar cone tree or a gingerbread person or two so they can be seen through your windows. A picture of a snowman hanging on the wall might be just enough to enchant a child looking in. Make it as elaborate or simple as you want—just remember, *now* is the time to do it.

In decorating the outside of the house, I suggest that you start with the walls (seams, doors, windows, and such). First cover the outside seams, where the cookie pieces come together, with icing dots, stars, or stripes. Once that's done, start working on the window and door designs, adding porch lights, doorbells, window garlands—whatever you fancy. Then do your roof and chimney. Keep the fence and yardwork until last; otherwise you'll get frustrated trying to dodge trees and bushes.

As you become more proficient, you'll have pretty much planned your house out ahead of time. You can decorate your house with all-white icing and candy, or mix up a batch each of red and green to add variety. If you decide to use colored icing, mix it up *before* you start to decorate. There's nothing worse than having an inspiration and having to postpone it while you color icing and fill a bag.

Decorating is definitely a matter of individual taste and experience. In this section I will give you numerous suggestions. I have divided the house into various architectural components and given you several different ways to handle each one. All of the methods I present are mix and match. Just let your imagination go. Whatever you choose will work very nicely.

Decorating Supplies

The following list of supplies is pretty comprehensive. You certainly don't need all these types of candy, or you may use others that you prefer. Look through the list and decide what you want on your particular house.

- Acrylic spray (or a good stiff hair spray will do in a pinch; *only* for inedible houses)

- Angel hair (*only* for inedible houses)

- CANDY

Candy canes (several 3-inch ones and a couple of 6-inch ones)

Gumdrops (small and large ones, all colors)

Life Saver candies

Necco Wafers

Party mix candy packs (with licorice pieces)

Peppermint candies (round, red and white)

Peppermint sticks (approx. 3 inches long)

Red and green candy dots (Red Hots)

Silver dragées (small silver dots used in cake decorating)

- Cellophane (clear or colored, for windows)

- Christmas ribbon (1-inch wide, or the depth of your baseboard)

- Glitter (real or edible—depending on whether you are going to eat your house)

- Sugar ice cream cones (with pointed end)

- Icing (white primarily—red/green/yellow optional)

- Pretzels (sticks and curved)

- Toothpicks (round wooden ones to make gumdrop trees or open clogged icing tips)

I've learned that chocolate candies do not hold up very well if you're planning to display the house year after year. They turn white and sometimes crack. Also, while candy-coated chocolates (such as M&M's) are very pretty, the candy coating has a tendency to crack and fall off after a few weeks. I'm not saying you shouldn't use this type candy (they make colorful and tasty decorations); just be aware of the possibilities and plan accordingly. Some hard candies become very sticky after a few weeks and their colors run. How do you know what types to use? Trial and error are the only teachers here. You'll just have to experiment.

I use an old pair of eyebrow tweezers to pick up very small candies (such as dragées or Red Hots) and place them on my house. That way, my fingers do not smash an icing dot or star.

Using the Decorating Tips

The decorating tips I recommended make a good basic set with which to do your house. If you've never decorated with icing tips, read the very general instructions on how to use the tips at the end of this section. However, a course in cake decorating at a local craft store is fun, inexpensive, and a great way to gain expertise. The course will give you a wide variety of methods for using decorating tips, but my instructions will get you started very nicely. Even a glance through a how-to-decorate-cakes book at the library will expand your talents. There's nothing very mysterious about cake decorating once you see how to do it. The four tips I've recommended—#3, #12, #16, and #21—can each be used in several ways.

#16 (SMALL STAR) AND #21 (LARGE STAR)
These tips can be used to make:

- single stars, with spaces between them

- stars in a row (no spaces between them)

- a scalloped running border (like seashells)

- a ridged solid line, straight or curved

- zigzag borders

#3 (SMALL DOT) AND #12 (LARGE DOT)
These tips can be used to make:

- large and small single dots

- connecting dots

- solid lines, curved or straight

- writing

The icing in the tips can dry out while you are decorating and make them impossible to work with. Unclog them by inserting a round wooden toothpick into the tip end. Be careful not to bend the tip while you are doing this. Covering your tips with a small piece of foil or plastic wrap also helps keep the icing from drying out—especially if you have several bags of icing in different colors filled and ready to go.

As you're decorating, occasionally wipe off the tip you're using with a paper towel. The tip will produce sharper decorations when it is clean.

If you have never used a decorating tube and tip before, here are a few hints.

1. Fill your bags only half to three-quarters full with icing.

2. Squeeze the bags from the top, not the middle, or you'll end up with icing all over your hands and none coming out of the tip. (I tie a twist tie around the end of the bag after I fill it and keep moving it down as I use the icing.)

3. To make a star or dot, place the tip, not quite touching the cookie, at a 90-degree angle to the surface. Gently squeeze (or pipe, the technical term) out the icing, lifting the tip slightly as you squeeze. When the star or dot is the size you want it, quit squeezing and lift the tip up and away from the surface. Position the tip for the next star or dot.

4. For continuous lines or to write, hold the tip, not quite touching the cookie, at a 45-degree angle to the surface. Squeeze the icing bag gently, with even pressure, and pull the tip along as you pipe.

Practice a bit on your countertop (kids love you to practice on their hands and arms; then they can eat off the icing) until you feel fairly comfortable with the procedure. If your hand shakes and you feel as if it may fall off after a couple of stars or dots, your icing is probably too stiff and needs to be thinned a bit. You'll need to remove the icing from the bag and add water—an ⅛ to a ¼ teaspoon at a time—until the icing is the consistency you want. Refill the bag and try again. After a while you'll be able to judge the proper viscosity of the icing before you fill the decorating bag. Keep in mind that a lot of decorating is going to tire out your hand—think of it as hand aerobics! You'll get stronger and better with practice.

General Information

I find that propping one side of my baseboard up on a book while I'm decorating is very helpful (see Figure 19). That way I

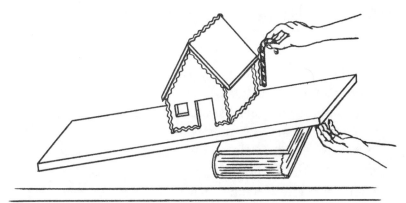

Fig. 19

Tilt the house so it's easier to decorate

don't have to be a contortionist to reach some areas, and it's a little easier to see what I'm doing.

Placing the entire baseboard (house and all) on a lazy susan or spinning tray (such as the kind for spices) is helpful as well. That way you can turn the house easily while you decorate.

Purchase a small piece of Styrofoam (12 by 12 inches is large enough) to use as a drying board for your accessories prior to gluing them on your house. Small accessories are less likely to get lost, crushed, or accidentally eaten if they're all in one area. For instance, I make several lollipop trees or sugar cone trees way before I'm ready to put them in the yard. In order to keep them fresh and undamaged, I stick them upright into the Styrofoam for safekeeping. If I decorate shutters, chimneys, or doors separately, I lay them on the drying board so that the decorating icing can dry to a hard finish *before* I glue them to the house. This little drying board is an invaluable tool that you can use over and over again.

To make your gingerbread house look its best, be sure that all raw edges have been decorated with little stars (#16), or little dots (#3), or something. Giving it that extra bit of attention makes it special. Think of it as hemming a dress. Without the hem, the dress is unfinished and you certainly wouldn't want to wear it in public that way. Of course, if your four-year-old is decorating, be thankful that the child has icing and candy on the house and not in her tummy or on your walls.

Attach a small candy cane or peppermint stick to each of the four corners of the house. These serve not only as decoration but also add structural strength to the house. *Make sure the candy is no taller than the side* of the house is high, or your roof won't fit correctly. To trim the candy sticks, score around them with a knife and then break the excess off with a quick snap. (In extreme cases of desperation, you can bite off the end.) When you attach the candy cane or peppermint stick, push the base of the candy into a pile of icing. Also squeeze a line of icing up the back of the candy and push it snugly against the corner of your house.

Not only do candy canes reinforce the structure and decorate the house, but if you decide to add a porch or small balcony (see "Other Accessories" on pages 70–77), they provide a superb base upon which the porch roof or balcony can sit. (See Figure 20.)

Decorative Components

There are numerous ways to decorate each architectural component, so pick what appeals to you. My goal is to get you started and give you various ideas. I know once you start decorating, you will come up with many other ideas. Please keep in mind that sometimes it is easier to decorate a house component before it's attached to the house. It really depends on how fancy the decorated piece is. The only difficulty with predecorated pieces is that you have to be extremely careful when attaching them. It's hard to hold a small, decorated shutter or door without smashing or knocking off a part of the icing or candy. But, conversely, sometimes it's very difficult to decorate that small shutter or door if it's already glued to the main frame. This area is one that you'll work out for yourself with

experience. I also suggest that you attach all the decorative components with decorating icing, even if you've assembled the house with a glue gun. Everything that goes on the main frame is very visible, and a glob of glue bulging out from behind a Life Saver porch light is not very pretty.

Doors

The easiest doors to make are those drawn directly onto the house with icing. Figures 21 to 23 are examples of doors you can draw on your house.

Doors can also be made of pretzel sticks glued onto the house. (See Figure 24.) About five pretzels snugged against one another, with a icing knob, make a very cute rustic-type back door. With your #16 (small star) or #3 (small dot) tip, outline the pretzel door with small stars or dots. In the center of each, put a small round candy (such as a Red Hot or silver dragée).

You also can make little doors of flat wafer cookies—the kind that come in chocolate, vanilla, and strawberry. If you use wafers, don't forget to decorate the raw edges.

The most elaborate doors are cut out from the dough either before the cookie is baked or as soon as the cookie comes out of the oven. Then you can decide which way you want the door to fit and prop it open a bit when you attach it to the house. To attach the door to the house, pipe a generous amount of icing up the hinge side of the cut-out door jamb and snug the door up to it. To decorate the door: Use a #3 (small dot) tip and draw a window on the door, or some cross beams, or attach a Life Saver and fill the hole with a white star

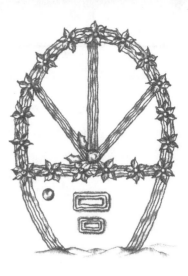

Fig. 20 (opposite)

Fig. 21 (below)

Fig. 22 (above)

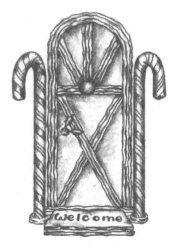

HINT:

Unless you're also planning to decorate the inside of your house, you probably don't want the door or the windows wide open. Remember, if you do get the urge to decorate the inside of your house, do so *before* you put the roof on.

Fig. 23

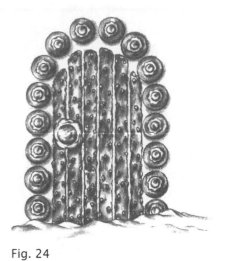

Fig. 24

Fig. 25

Fig. 26

GINGERBREAD HOUSES

for a window. Use the #16 (small star) tip to make a doorknob, and put a silver dragée in the center of the knob for added effect. With the #3 or #16 tip, pipe an edging around the cut edge of the door to finish it off. (See Figure 25.)

Doors also can be a combination of cut-out and drawn on (for instance, a dutch door). The top half is slightly open and the bottom is half drawn on. (See Figure 26.)

$\mathcal{W}$INDOWS

Windows, like doors, can be cut out at baking time. I use cookie cutters in the shape of stars, squares, diamonds, circles, and the like. (See Figures 27 to 29.) Or you can just take a paring knife and cut a window into the dough before you bake it. If you decide on cut out windows, remove the window dough before you bake or the dough will bake together again and

Fig. 27

Diamond cookie cutter

Fig. 28

Round cookie cutter (left)

Fig. 29

Star cookie cutter (right)

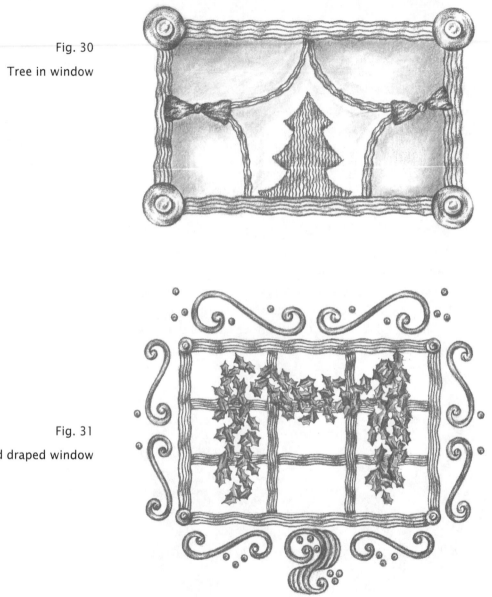

Fig. 30
Tree in window

Fig. 31
Garland draped window

GINGERBREAD HOUSES

you'll have a nice outline of the window, but no opening. Sometimes that's what you want, though. If it is, stamp your dough with the cookie cutter *prior* to baking and use the resulting outline as a decorating guide.

With #16 (small star) or #3 (small dot) tip, outline the windows with closely spaced stars or dots. Put a small Red Hot in the corner stars or dots. Draw frames on your windows with white icing.

In one drawn-in window (the front of the house window, perhaps), pipe a Christmas tree with green icing stars (see Figure 30), or drape the inside of the window with a garland. (See Figure 31.) (See "Wreaths and Garlands" on page 75 for the proper technique.)

Start at the center of a round window, and with the #3 (small dot) tip, draw a line spiraling out. Keep going round and round until you meet the outer edge of the window. Draw five lines from the center point to suggest a spiderweb design. With the #16 (small star) tip, make a single star in the center of the window and top the star with a red hot (or green hot). (See Figure 32.)

Around a round window, draw a wreath. (See page 75 for the technique.)

If your windows are cut out and you haven't put glass (see below) in them, glue a decorated gingerbread girl or boy cookie against the inside of the window as if it's looking out. Even a gingerbread bear would be cute this way.

Window Glass If you want glass in your windows, before you

Fig. 32

Spider window

assemble the house, cover the inside of each window with colored cellophane (the kind used to wrap fruit baskets). Use your glue gun or icing to stick the cellophane to the cookie. If you want your windows to look opaque, use stenciling plastic. This will allow the light to shine through but make it impossible to see into the house. Or you can use candy glass (recipe follows)—this is especially nice if the house is to be eaten.

CANDY GLASS

Preheat the oven to 250° F.

1. Cover a cookie sheet with foil wrap. Give the foil a very light greasing with vegetable oil or shortening.

2. Put several Life Savers (or any transparent colored, hard candy) in a zip-locked bag. With a rolling pin, crush the candy to a fine powder. Try to crush every thing uniformly—otherwise you'll end up with lumpy windows. If you're making a lot of candy glass, use a food processor or blender to grind the candies.

3. Sprinkle the candy powder evenly on the foil-lined cookie sheet. Make certain you have spread the powder thickly enough so that you can't see the foil under the candy easily and that there are no large gaps or thin spots. The area that you cover with the candy powder will pretty much be the size of window glass—the powder doesn't spread much.

4. Place the cookie sheet in the preheated oven. Keep a *very close* watch on the melting candy—it can burn easily. In a couple of minutes, the candy should have melted completely and have become a thin, shiny, hard layer.

5. Remove the cookie sheet from the oven and let it cool thoroughly (just a few minutes). Then very carefully remove the foil from the candy layer.

6. Then break (again, carefully) the candy to the size you need to cover a window. Use icing to attach the candy to the inside of the window. When you are decorating your window, you can pipe window frames directly onto the candy glass.

These "glass" sheets are very delicate and require a light touch, but the results are stunning. Stained glass made with this method (sprinkle different colors onto the foil) is so pretty that no one will want to eat it.

The only problem I've encountered with windows of this type is that they will melt if the weather gets too warm. Consequently, they're not good to use in houses that are to be kept past one season. A small light in the house doesn't seem to hurt the windows, however. Apparently, the light doesn't generate enough heat to affect the candy glass.

CHIMNEY

Chimneys can be made in several different ways: You can bake a chimney, you can use a sugar ice cream cone, or you can build a chimney of store-bought cookies or candy. I've included a pattern for one type of chimney that works on any house with a slanted roof. (See Figure 2 on page 8.) The primary thing to remember about chimneys, whether you bake them from scratch or make them out of cookies or cones, is that they have to have a V notch on the bottom to set it over the V on the roof. Or you can make the base of the chimney at a slant so it will sit along the slant of your roof as the chimney pattern in this book does. (See Figure 2.)

There are a number of ways to decorate your chimney.

Fig. 34

Spire chimney (opposite)

Fig. 33

Star chimney (below)

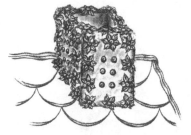

You can completely frost your chimney with red icing (thin the icing down a bit so it spreads smoothly) and then place cut red or black licorice strings on the chimney to make a bricklike pattern. Arrange the licorice strings on the chimney before the icing dries so that they are glued on tightly.

Another method is to use white icing and the #16 (small star) tip to pipe rows of stars around the top edges of the chimney, down each of the seams, and around the base where the chimney attaches to the house. With red and green icing and the #3 (small dot) tip, scatter red and green dots all over the sides of the chimney, inside the white star border. (See Figure 33.)

To change the house into a church, you can place a sugar ice cream cone on the front part of the roof as a steeple. Use white icing and the #3 (small dot) tip to pipe small white dots over the entire steeple. Place a silver dragée in the center of

each dot. Using the #21 (large star) tip, top the steeple with a large star. (See Figure 34.)

You can carefully saw your chimney pattern pieces out of plain graham crackers instead of baking them from gingerbread dough. Use a serrated knife and a light touch to cut the graham crackers. Assemble the chimney with white icing, then leave it natural except for adding an icing snowfall trim over the top edges. Pull some of the snow down to simulate icicles.

Still another method is to use sugar wafers to build a small chimney. Place it at the very back edge of the roof. Glue more wafers under the chimney, down the back of the house, to make a fireplace chimney from the bottom to the top floor. Be sure to finish the raw edges on the fireplace brickwork as well as the chimney.

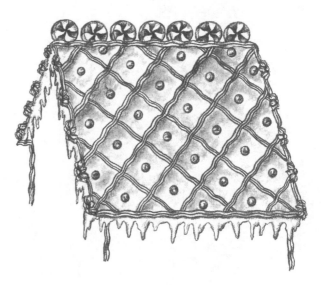

Fig. 35

Peppermint pinwheel roof

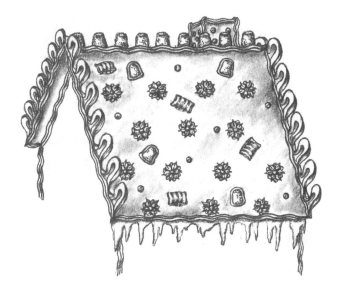

Fig. 36
Candy and star roof

ROOF

The roof of your house is a lot of fun to decorate. After you decide where you would like your chimney placed, decide how to decorate the roof.

At the peak of your roof, where the two roof pieces meet, squeeze out a row of large stars with the #21 (large star) tip. You can leave these stars plain, or add a Red Hot, or a small gumdrop or a round peppermint candy (set upright on its rim) to each star. Regardless of how simply or elaborately you decorate this area, make sure you put some icing where the two roof pieces meet to help stabilize the house. (See Figures 35 and 36.)

On the roof surface itself, use your #21 (large star) tip to

DECORATING YOUR HOUSE

drop snow all over in a random pattern. The #21 tip gives the drops personality. Then push some small and large gumdrops, licorice pieces, or red/green hots into the icing snow.

If you know how to make a shell with your icing tips (usually #16 and #21), frame your roof with shells, then add a colored dot or small candy to each shell center.

With the #21 (large star) tip, pipe a scallop design on the roof. Add a Red Hot where the scallops meet each other. Or, if you have colored icing made up, alternate small dots of red and green along the scalloped design. (See Figure 37.)

Roofs can also be left plain and snow-covered. Starting at the peak of the roof, just pile the icing on with a knife. Push the snow down the roof to the bottom edges. Some of it could hang over the eaves for a more authentic look as well as to hide the raw roof edges.

If you're willing to live with many crumbs, make a straw

Fig. 37

Scalloped roof

Fig. 38

Star chimney and
shredded wheat roof

thatched roof. (See Figure 38.) Take a box of miniature Shredded Wheat biscuits. Cut them in half to make the biscuit thinner, and, starting at the eaves (bottom) edge of the roof, glue a row of half biscuits across the roof. When you glue on the second row of thatching, make sure to overlap the top of the first row of biscuits just a little. Keep adding rows until you reach the peak of the roof. Then repeat up the other roof side. It's important that you start at the bottom edge of the roof. You can attach a final row of biscuits where the two pieces of roof meet at the peak, or you can trim the peak with large stars, dots, or shells of icing. If you use frosted biscuits, you'll get a snowy roof.

If the idea of crumbs everywhere revolts you, use the same shingling technique just described, but use flat, wafer-type

DECORATING YOUR HOUSE

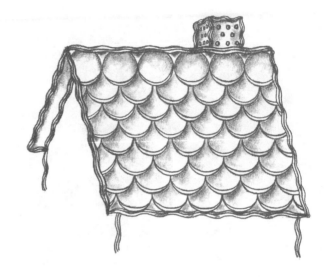

Fig. 39

Neccos roof

candies (such as Neccos) instead. (See Figure 39.) Be somewhat careful here, though. Candy is heavy. Neccos work okay,
but if you get an urge to use candy pieces that are heavier—say
1 to 2 inches in diameter and 1/2 inch thick—you're probably
going to have to bake a new roof, because the weight of the
candy will have caved in this one.

Other Accessories

Shutters

Shutters for your windows can be made out of small pieces of
gingerbread, cut when you are cutting your original house
pieces (see Figure 40).

Fig. 40

GIngerbread shutters

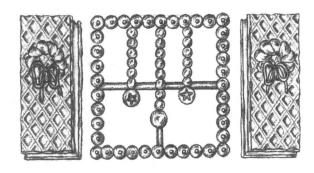

Fig. 41

Wafer cookie shutters

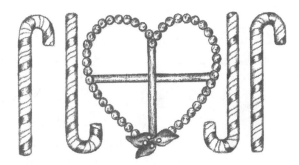

Fig. 42

Candy shutters

DECORATING YOUR HOUSE

You can saw down wafer-type cookies to make shutters. (See Figure 41.)

Flat, large pieces of candy make good shutters also, or even small candy canes. (See Figure 42.)

Fig. 43

Gum shutters

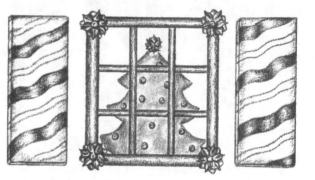

Pieces of gum (preferably the striped kind) are very colorful as shutters and are easily trimmed to size. (See Figure 43.)

Don't forget to decorate your shutters and finish the raw edges.

STEPS AND RAILINGS

If you want steps coming from your front door, be sure to draw or cut out the front door about ⅜ inch up from the bottom of the cookie piece. This will allow you to have a three-step staircase. To make your steps at baking time, cut out of the dough three small rectangles that are at least ¼ inch longer than your door is wide. Each rectangle should also be an ⅛ inch narrower than the last one. For example—if your door width is about 1¼ inches, your first step should be 1½ inches wide by 1¼ inches deep, the second step should be 1½ inches wide by 1⅛ inches deep, and the top should be 1½ inches wide by 1 inch deep. After baking the pieces, use your emery board to even out the edges. Then glue your steps together, making sure the backs of the steps are aligned so that you can place the glued-together piece snugly against your house. (See Figure 44.) You really don't have to finish the raw edges of steps—they have a rustic look anyway. Sometimes I outline them in icing, though, to make them really show up.

You can make steps any size you want using the basic proportions just given. Make them wider and deeper and you could have a porch on your house. This is especially nice if you have a balcony (see "Balconies" on page 74), because the balcony then serves as a roof for the porch.

Make railings by stacking little candies to make posts (use your icing to glue the candies together) and then, with white icing, cement pretzel sticks across the tops of the posts.

You also can make posts from pretzel sticks that have been cut down to size.

Or use candy that is already shaped like fence or railing posts, such as candy-coated licorice pieces that come in pink, white, and black. Glue licorice strings across the tops of these candy posts as railings.

Fig. 44

Steps, railings

Fig. 45
Balconies

ℬALCONIES

Balconies are easy to make and install. When you're cutting out your house, cut a rectangle out of cookie dough that is at least 1 inch wide and about ½ inch shorter than the length of your front and back pieces. After it's baked, you can trim it with a knife or use your emery board to even out the side that will be against the house.

Pipe a generous amount of icing onto one long edge of the balcony and press it against the house wall over the front door. You're going to have to brace up the balcony until the icing sets. To give the balcony more strength, I suggest that you lay it over a couple of peppermint sticks glued upright to the house sides directly under it. They look pretty and make the balcony very stable.

If you decide to make a wide balcony (or an upstairs deck), put peppermint stick columns along each front corner of the deck. (See Figure 45.) Decorate each column with a garland. (See "Wreaths and Garlands" below.)

Draw French doors on your house wall behind the balcony, and decorate each window pane with a tiny Christmas wreath.

Decorate your balcony with a licorice-string railing (see page 73), small bushes, flower pots, and the like. (See page 84.)

$\mathcal{W}$REATHS AND $\mathcal{G}$ARLANDS

Wreaths and garlands draped over windows and doors and around mailboxes or lampposts add a festive touch to any gingerbread house. (See Figure 46.)

To make a wreath, use green icing and a #16 (small star) tip to pipe stars, touching each other, in a circle directly onto your house where you wish the wreath to be. Make a second row of stars around the outside of the first. (If your wreath is tiny—in a window, for instance—one row might be enough.)

Use red icing and the #3 (small dot) tip to pipe red spots onto your green wreath to look like holly berries. Then, with white icing, draw a bow on the wreath.

To make a garland, follow the same techniques you used to make a wreath except, instead of a circle of stars, loop a single line of touching stars over a doorway or a window. A garland around a lamppost or mailbox post is nice also.

$\mathcal{B}$ELLS

Gumdrop bells look cute over windows or doors. If you use yellow gumdrops, they give the impression of a lamp. Red gumdrops look like Christmas bells, especially with a white icing bow on them. Experiment until you find what you really like best.

To make a bell ensemble, you'll need three half gumdrops. Cut two small gumdrops in half lengthwise. Look at the gumdrop halves. With the rounded part as the top and a bit of pushing, they look just like little bells. Eat one of the halves. Glue one other half (sticky side against the house) at a slight angle with the rounded top part pointing toward the center of the house. Glue another half gumdrop to the right of the first one at a slight angle the other way. The rounded part should be touching the left gumdrop. Cut the last half gumdrop with a knife so that it's a little skinnier than the other two halves. Using a generous amount of icing, glue this skinny half on top of the other two halves. Hold it there until the gumdrop stays by itself (a minute or so). Once the bells are set, outline them in icing with a #3 (small dot) tip. Add a small dot of icing un-

Fig. 47

Gumdrop bells (above)

Fig. 46 (opposite)

DECORATING YOUR HOUSE

der each bell as a clapper and draw a bow over the top of the bells. (See Figure 47.)

Anchoring Accessories

When you get to the landscaping of your gingerbread house, you'll have to anchor various accessories such as trees, lampposts, and mailboxes. How you anchor them depends on the type of baseboard you have chosen.

STYROFOAM BASE

If you are using a Styrofoam base, start by deciding where you want the accessories to be. Then make a hole in the Styrofoam large enough to accommodate whatever you will be placing in the yard. Pipe some white icing into the hole, position the post or trunk in the hole, and hold it there until the icing sets a bit. If you made the hole too large and your tree, mailbox, or lamppost is just not going to stand upright, break off some short lengths of wooden toothpicks and wedge them around the post to brace it. Add more icing to cement the whole thing together. Don't worry about the toothpicks showing; you'll eventually cover them with snow.

OTHER TYPES OF BASES

If you're using a base that you can't dig into (cardboard, a serving tray, whatever), you'll need to anchor your posted objects with Life Savers, large gumdrops, or a mound of decorating

Fig. 48

Life Saver pot with a gumdrop flower

78

icing. Actually, the Life Saver anchoring method works best. Gumdrops will split if the post is too large, and decorating icing has to be baby-sat while it dries.

To anchor with the Life Savers, stack and glue three to four Life Savers together, making sure the holes are aligned. Now cement the Life Saver stack to the baseboard with icing. When the stack is dry and stable, fill the hole with icing, insert the post, and hold it steady until the icing sets. This works very well if your post is a thin pretzel stick or lollipop stick. If your post is tall, you may need to add a few more Life Savers to the stack. Again, if the hole is too large, wedge it with broken toothpicks, but mask them this time as the stack will most likely be above your snow line. (See Figure 48.)

MAILBOX

Mailboxes are the pièce de résistance of your gingerbread house. People will love your gingerbread houses, but when they see your mailboxes, they'll go crazy. You can personalize the mailboxes with a name or a house number. If you are making a gingerbread house for a gift, this personalization makes it very special. Keep in mind, however, that a name with more than seven letters or numerous fat letters (a, b, c, m, and so on), just won't fit onto this mailbox. If necessary, put the name on a cookie doormat—it has more room and is still special. The mailbox, then, becomes a great place for just the house number. Or, for generic giving, "North Pole" (two lines), "Santa," or "Mail" also work very nicely on the mailbox. (See Figure 49.)

Fig. 49

Tootsie Roll mail box

To make a basic mailbox, you will need the following:

- 1 small Tootsie Roll–type candy (not the really tiny ones, but the ones that are the next step up in size)

- A pretzel stick to make the mailbox post

- White, red, and green icing

- #3 (small dot) and

- #16 (small star) tips

The procedure is somewhat complicated. I'll break it down into steps here.

1. Use your fingers to squeeze the candy roll into the approximate shape of a regular mailbox. Stretch it a bit if the name you need to write is a long one. The warmth from your hands generally is enough to soften the candy and make it malleable. If the candy is too firm to work with, microwave it for 2 to 3 seconds. Be very careful if you do: Sugar gets extremely hot in the microwave and, even though the roll may look intact, the inside becomes molten sugar if microwaved for too long. Not only will the candy be useless as a mailbox, but it also can blister your skin. If you overheat your first candy, let it cool and eat it. Then try again with a new candy.

2. Use a toothpick (or a nut pick—it doesn't break as eas-

ily) to make a hole in the bottom center of the mail-box-shape roll. You might have to reshape a bit after you've dug the hole. This hole should be large enough to accommodate a pretzel stick. Squeeze some icing into the hole and insert the pretzel stick. Hold the stick straight for a minute or so (or lay the candy on your drying board, stick up) until the icing has set and the candy is no longer in jeopardy of falling off.

3. After the mailbox is secure, hold the pretzel stick, and outline the ends of the mailbox with white icing using a #3 (small dot) tip. Also, write the name on the box at this point. If you run out of room or make a mistake, don't panic. Just wipe off the icing and try again. A toothpick and a damp eye makeup sponge applicator clean up mistakes very well.

4. With red icing and a #3 (small dot) tip, pipe a red flag onto one side of the box.

5. With green icing and a #16 (small star) tip, pipe a garland of green stars halfway down the pretzel stick. Start right under the mailbox where the candy roll and the pretzel stick meet. Then put some red berries on the garland with a #3 (small dot) tip. (See "Wreaths and Garlands" on page 75 for the proper technique.)

6. When you're ready to landscape your gingerbread house, anchor the mailbox to the baseboard. (See "Anchoring Accessories" on page 78.) Make a note of how tall your mailbox will sit once anchored. Usually

the pretzel stick is too tall for verisimilitude. I personally nibble my mailbox post down to size.

$\mathcal{W}$OODPILE

As with mailboxes, woodpiles create a chorus of oohs and ahs.
Unlike the mailboxes, however, woodpiles are very easy and
quick to make. (See Figure 50.)

All you need to do is break thin, straight pretzel sticks into
various lengths (½ to 2 inches).

Then, using white icing as glue, pile these logs next to the
house 5 or 6 logs deep and ending in kind of a pyramid of
logs. Scatter a few around.

The icing will look like snow between the logs. Put some
snow on the top of the logs and pull some icing down from the
ends of the logs to look like icicles.

Fig. 50

Voilá—a woodpile

GINGERBREAD HOUSES

ℒAMPPOSTS

To make a lamppost, push a large yellow gumdrop onto a peppermint stick (not too deep or the gumdrop will split). Secure it with icing. You'll have to hold the peppermint stick and gumdrop until icing sets. (See Figure 51.)

Another cute lamppost can be made by pushing the curved end of a candy cane into a yellow Life Saver hole. Add icing over and under the Life Saver hole to secure the candies. If you want more light, glue two Life Savers together and then attach them with icing to the candy cane. (See Figure 52.)

With white icing, attach a yellow Life Saver or a yellow gumdrop directly onto the house, either over or beside the door, to make a great porch light.

Fig. 51

Peppermint stick post and a gumdrop light (left)

Fig. 52

Candy cane post and a Life Saver lamp (below)

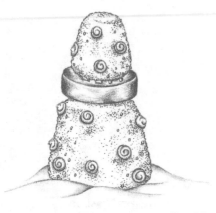

Fig. 53

Gumdrop and Life Saver bush
(above)

Fig. 54

Lollipop trees (below)

Bushes and Trees

Be generous with your plantings around the house. Bushes and trees add a lot of atmosphere to the scene. Small gumdrop bushes right next to the house can frame windows or doors or can be stacked up (use toothpicks to hold the gumdrops together) as minitrees. Be creative—use a purple gumdrop and pipe red dots onto it. It's whimsical, which is what a gingerbread house should be.

Push a round, wooden toothpick into the top center of a large gumdrop, leaving plenty of toothpick showing above the top of the gumdrop. Slide a Life Saver onto the toothpick on top of the gumdrop, then push a small gumdrop onto the toothpick over the Life Saver. Stop here for a bush. Break off any toothpick showing at the top or push it into the baseboard when you plant your yard. If you'd like a tree, keep adding Life Savers and gumdrops to the toothpick. Put icing dots all over the gumdrops. (See Figure 53.)

For a cute little tree in a pot, glue three Life Saver candies in a stack, making sure the holes are aligned. Set it aside for a moment. Now, with a toothpick, make a hole in the bottom of a large or small gumdrop, so that you can push it onto a pretzel stick. Dab a bit of icing around the hole to secure the pretzel to the gumdrop. Fill the Life Saver stack hole with icing and insert the pretzel stick with the gumdrop on the top.

You can make cute trees using small round lollipops and icing. With your #3 (small dot) tip and icing (any color), make small dots all over one lollipop, squiggles over another colored one; a never-ending spiral over another, and so on. Use these lollipops in clusters of three as a little grove of trees. Vary their height by cutting some of the trunks down with a knife. If you prefer green trunks, wrap the lollipop sticks in florist tape. (See Figure 54.)

Trees also can be made from very tall lollipops (such as unicorn pops—see Figure 55). Just push them into your Styrofoam base.

To make a triangular tree, squeeze a generous amount of

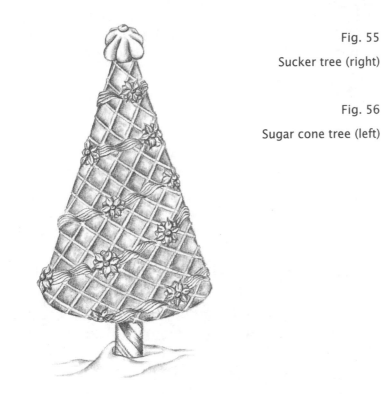

Fig. 55

Sucker tree (right)

Fig. 56

Sugar cone tree (left)

icing inside the tip of a sugar ice cream cone. Insert a peppermint candy stick longer than the cone is high (no hook) into the cone, and embed it in the icing. The cone is your tree, the candy stick is the trunk. Pipe small stars or dots all over the cone. Add a large star (use tip #21) to the point of the cone and top with a Red Hot. (See Figure 56.)

You can make another triangular tree using a sugar cone on which you pipe little stars, very close together, using green icing and a #16 (small star) tip. Add red icing berries for decoration. These trees can be just set on the baseboard, or you can add a peppermint candy stick trunk to them. If you want a short tree, cut down the sugar cone and/or the tree trunk.

FENCES

Important: Put the fence in your yard as you're snowing the yard. (See "Snow" on page 89.) A fence around your gingerbread house yard frames the completed work and adds character to the overall design. Fences can be built in an unlimited number of ways. You can stack up, line up, or stick together *anything* to make a fence. Keep your fence (whatever it's made of) at least a quarter inch in from the edge of the baseboard. A fence flush with the edge makes picking up the house without breaking the fence difficult, plus someone is more likely to run into the fence when the house is being displayed.

Don't forget, most fences have a gate. Gates are useful if you're making a pattern in your fence and don't quite have enough room for that last pattern. That's a good place for a gate! Here are a few ideas for fences.

Alternate large gumdrops with rounded (approximately 2-inch size) pretzels. Use all different color gumdrops. (See Figure 57.)

Or use a line of small rounded pretzels—single hump down—all by themselves for a fence. Put white icing on the rounded tops of the pretzels to simulate snow.

Fig. 57

Pretzel and gumdrop fence

Use pretzel sticks as posts. Break the pretzels to about 2-inch lengths and anchor each one in a pile of snow. Glue pretzel sticks along the top of these posts. Don't forget to *measure* the railing pretzel sticks so you can space the posts correctly. (See Figure 58.)

For a more colorful variation on this idea, use small gum-

Fig. 58

Pretzel fence

Fig. 59

Tootsie Roll candy fences

drops as posts and glue pretzel-stick railings along the tops of the gumdrops.

Alternate round peppermint candies (1-inch size) with Tootsie Roll posts. (See Figure 59.)

Fig. 60

Candy cane fences

Use small candy canes to frame a piece of round peppermint candy. (See Figure 60.)

$\mathcal{I}$CICLES

The icing you use to make the icicles and snow on your gingerbread house needs to be somewhat thinner than the icing you use for the other decorating. I suggest you combine the white icing remaining in the tube with any leftover white icing. Then, depending on how stiff the icing is and how much you've got left, beat water or white corn syrup (1 teaspoon at a time) into the icing. The corn syrup does two things: (1) It thins the icing so that the icicles and snow come out very, very smooth, and (2) it makes the icing shiny when it dries. Don't make the icing too thin—while it needs to flow easily off the decorator tip, it should still hold its shape when piled up.

Use your #3 (small dot) tip and your rebeaten, thinned icing to put icicles on your house. I find framing the eaves of the roof with the icicles looks best. Starting at one corner of the roof eaves, push the tip up the cookie from below (maybe under some icing if you've already snowed your roof) and pipe a generous amount of icing onto the gingerbread. This is your anchor. Still squeezing, slowly pull the tube down and away from the house, causing the icing to elongate into an icicle. When you quit squeezing and keep pulling, the icicle will break off. Don't worry if some icicles are short and some are long—this adds to the authentic look of icicle formation. You'll get the feel of making icicles with very little practice. Just remember to give each icicle a good anchor. Repeat the process around the house.

Don't forget to put a few icicles on your woodpile, on bushes, railings, across the balcony . . .

$\mathcal{S}$NOW

Using a small butter knife or a putty knife, and working from the house toward the outer edge of the baseboard, spread the remaining icing onto the yard a small section at a time. Push some of the icing up onto the corners and walls of the house to give the appearance of snowdrifts, and dab a bit on the foundation plantings around the windows and doors. As you're putting the snow in your yard, assemble the fence. The icing will secure the fence and will look more natural than if you attempt to work it around a prepositioned object. The icing will dry very hard, so run your knife around the edge of the baseboard every so often to clean off any snow that hangs over.

Finishing Touches

It's the final, little things that make your house so very special. It's like framing a picture or adding flowers to a table—not really necessary, but oh so pleasing when it's done. Be careful though. If you have made your gingerbread house to eat, you can't use some of these items. I've marked the ones to avoid if the house is to be nibbled upon—smoke made from angel hair, inedible glitter, and spraying. If your house will be strictly for decoration, all of the ideas here may be used to add that final magic to your house.

Smoke

To create the illusion of smoke from your chimney, use angel hair or cotton. But a big, big caution here: **Angel hair is made of spun glass! Do not use it on a house you will eat.**

If your house is for decoration only, take a small amount of angel hair and fold it over so that it is very wispy. Squeeze some icing into the hollow of the chimney and, using a pencil, push the end of the angel hair into the chimney, embedding it in the icing. After the icing sets, spread the fold of angel hair so it looks as if the smoke is blowing.

Angel hair is usually a seasonal item. Most of the time it can be found only during the Christmas season in stores that carry holiday ornaments and trims. However, large craft outlets may carry it, especially if they have year-round holiday displays for their crafters. A box of angel hair is quite inexpensive and will last practically forever. I bought a box about five years ago and still have some left over, and I've made many smoking chimneys during those five years.

If you simply can't find angel hair or are concerned about little ones trying to eat or play with it, use white cotton instead. You can pull the cotton out to a configuration resembling smoke. It's not as wispy as angel hair and doesn't have the sheen, but perhaps it will relieve you of some anxiety if there are small children around.

$\mathcal{E}$DIBLE AND $\mathcal{I}$NEDIBLE $\mathcal{G}$LITTER

Edible Glitter Edible glitter (you *can* eat it) may be found in any shop that carries cake decorating equipment. It comes in a variety of colors, though I personally like white best. Sprinkle this glitter onto the icing while you are snowing your house so that it will stick. But beware. There is a fine line between melting your edible glitter (because the snow is too wet) and having it sparkle. Once again, trial and error are the best teachers here.

Coarse, colored sugar also can be used for glitter. Melted blue sugar can turn into a lovely duck pond or ice skating rink in your yard. (To melt the sugar, follow the basic directions for making candy glass on pages 62–63; omitting steps 1 and 2.) Like edible glitter, this sugar is generally found in specialty stores that carry cake decorating supplies. It's a little hard to find, but it's such fun to use that it's worth the hunt.

Inedible Glitter Inedible glitter (you *cannot* eat it) may be found in any craft shop. Again, it comes in a variety of colors. I suggest you use the white or clear. This glitter comes in different textures or grains (from very fine to somewhat coarse). I prefer using the coarser grain as it seems to sparkle more. Because inedible (craft) glitter is made of an acrylic or plastic, it will not melt as you apply it to your house. In fact, it will last for a very long time. The major hazard with this glitter is that it may blow off.

The best time to apply inedible glitter is while you are spraying acrylic sealer (see the next section, on acrylic sealer) on your house. The sealer acts as an adhesive, and there will be less shedding of sparklies. You must, however, spray first, then sprinkle glitter. If you attempt to spray *after* you apply the glitter, the spray will blow off the glitter and also dull it.

If you place a couple sheets of newspaper under your house while you are glittering, you'll be able to gather up wayward glitter to use for future projects. Be generous with the glitter. Put some in a small bowl and use your fingers to sprinkle it on. You'll waste less and have more control over where it's going than if you just sprinkle from the jar or bowl.

$\mathcal{A}$CRYLIC $\mathcal{S}$EALER

Attention: The acrylic sealer spray is not to be ingested— follow the instructions on the can! If you are going to eat your house, do not spray the house or any of its components.

If you wish to keep your house year after year, I highly recommend that you spray the entire house (decorations and all) with an acrylic sealer. By doing so, your house will retain its colors and overall appearance longer.

Acrylic sprays come in matte or glossy finishes. Use whichever one you'd like as the spray has no discernible affect on the house or its decorations (unless, of course, you apply several coats—which is unnecessary and expensive).

The sealer can be purchased in any craft store and comes under many different brand names. Look for one that is recommended to artists—usually such a spray will not cause the colors to run. Acrylic sealers come out in a very fine mist. Besides protecting the house from deterioration, the spray also will discourage any bugs attracted by the sweet smell of icing and cookie from camping in your house.

Let your house dry for at least four to six hours before you spray.

The directions on the can suggest (among other things) that you hold your breath while using the spray. I find this difficult, but I do open all the surrounding windows and make sure not to spray into anyone's face. The spray will get onto everything in the immediate area if you're not very careful. The best way to prevent this from happening is to create an enclosure in which to spray the house. To do so, cut off the top and one side of a large cardboard carton. Set your house in the box (as if on a stage) to spray it. This enclosure will keep the spray on the gingerbread house and in the box—two excellent places for it. If all else fails, take your house into the garage to spray it (away from the cars, please) or, if it's not raining or snowing or windy, spray outside. But watch for any temperature constraints outlined on the can.

Do not spray over glitter; the spray will dull it. Apply glitter immediately *after* you've sprayed. The acrylic spray dries fast, so work with small areas at a time. I've found that it's best to start at the roof of the house, lightly spray a small area, then immediately sprinkle glitter over that area. Spray another small area and glitter it, so on and so forth, turning the house as you move progressively down toward the yard area.

When you spray, pay particular attention to covering all the silver dragées if you've used any. Unless they are coated with acrylic, after a few days, all the silver coating will tarnish or turn black. I've also coated them with clear nail polish to keep them from turning color. Of course, that's when I know the house is not going to get eaten.

Any acrylic spray is expensive. However, one can will last a very long time. I have sprayed at least twenty to twenty-five houses with the last can I purchased.

Ribbon and Bows

If you're using a Styrofoam baseboard, use your glue gun to glue decorative ribbon around the perimeter of your baseboard, the last raw edge on your creation. Use ribbon with Christmas plaid designs, red ribbon with gold or silver flake, or just plain red or green ribbon. "Velvet" ribbon, while very pretty, is ex-

94

tremely difficult to glue because the nap comes off when the wet glue hits it. Patterned rayon ribbon works best. Buy it by the spool. Craft stores have periodic sales on ribbon and you can pick up very nice quality goods for a minimal price.

Finally, make a small bow and glue it to the front of the baseboard.

$\mathcal{L}$IGHTING

As mentioned earlier, the time to think about whether your house will be lighted is *before* you assemble it. Once the house is glued to the baseboard, making a hole in the baseboard to accommodate the light is very difficult. It will be *impossible* to make that hole without breaking the gingerbread cookies if the roof is in place.

If you have decided that you want your house lighted, your next important decision revolves around the type of base the house will be sitting on. If you use a something other than a Styrofoam base, you're going to have to figure out how to set the light in the house and how to replace the bulbs when they burn out. This requires tools and supplies that are generally found in the garage (drills, screws, duct tape, and so on)— much too involved for your first effort. So, if you want to light your first house, please use a Styrofoam base. These instructions will assume that's what you have chosen.

I find it easiest to purchase a complete lighting set (bulb, base, and cord) at a craft shop—they'll run under $5 in most stores. Ask for the sets used in nightlight ceramics with a

squeezable base (usually made of a lightweight metal) instead of the screw-in kind. The bulbs in this type are easier to change because you can pinch the base and easily pull it through a hole in the Styrofoam. The bases use Christmas tree light bulbs or nightlight bulbs, so don't worry about replacing them when the light burns out. For a different effect on the finished house, try changing the color of the bulb. Red is pretty, so is blue.

The basic steps in lighting your house are:

1. Cut out the windows *before* you bake your house.

2. Decide if you want glass (cellophane, plastic, or candy—see pages 59–62) in your windows *before* you assemble the house. You can also leave the windows empty, without any covering. Keep in mind, however, that if you use clear cellophane or leave your windows empty, everyone will be able to look inside your house. Are you decorating the inside also?

3. Determine where on your baseboard you'll want the light. Then, using a quarter as an outline (that seems to be the right size for the lights I purchase), cut a hole large enough to accommodate the light set through the Styrofoam base. You'll want to make sure the bulb will be secure and sit above the Styrofoam a bit so it doesn't melt or burn it.

4. You have two options now. On the bottom side of the Styrofoam base, you can carve a channel for the cord

extending from the hole for the light toward the back of the house. You don't want a cord sticking out from under the front of the baseboard. The channel will keep your house flat on the table instead of rolling on the lighting cord.

Another method is to make Styrofoam "feet" for your baseboard. (See Figure 61.) These feet will not only allow the cord to lie unobstructed, but will come in handy even if the house is unlit. (See page 20.)

5. Now assemble your house. The light can be inserted or removed at will, so put it aside until you are ready to display the finished gingerbread house.

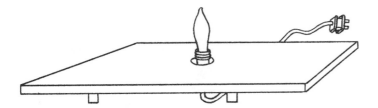

Fig. 61

A lighted base

8.
Storing

Can you believe it—the season is over. The house was a tremendous success. A lot of work, but fun work. Young and old alike were enchanted with the candy bells and lollipop trees and, are still talking about the little woodpile in the backyard. You've even managed to keep the neighbor's toddler from eating all the icicles off the house. (That's okay. You can do icicle touchups when you bring the house out next holiday season.) Now the question is: How do we store this masterpiece? Here are some basic rules that will ensure that you'll have a lovely house again next year.

First, your house will keep best if it is stored in an even-temperatured environment, for instance in a closet. The temperature in attics and basements tends to go to extremes during the year, and the house will not stand up to great fluctuations.

Second, your house needs some air. A completely sealed environment (unless sterile) will encourage the growth of mildew and mold. What disgusting things they are!

So with those ideas in mind, here's how to store your house.

At a minimum, place your house into a large, plastic garbage sack. Secure the top. Poke a few breathing holes in it and place your masterpiece on the top shelf of the least-used closet in the house. This works very nicely if you don't have to worry about someone knocking it over or crushing it while looking for the slides you took during last year's New Year's Eve party.

An even better solution is to find a box that will accommodate the width of the baseboard and the height of the house. You don't want the box so large that the house slides around in it; a ¼-inch clearance is plenty. Close the lid, label the box in very big letters, and put it on the top shelf of the closet. The house will be just fine until next holiday season.

If you have pets, do *not* store your house on the floor or bottom shelf of anything. We had a dog that licked every Necco walkway stone down to the Styrofoam base in one season. No wonder she got so fat!

After a Year

When you take your house out for another year, you may have to do some minor maintenance. For instance, maybe little Jimmy next door picked off all the icicles off the left roof. Whip up some icing (a half batch will do) and replace those missing icicles. Maybe your fence has a broken pretzel or knocked-over post. Use that icing and mend away.

Once you've fixed the house, you notice that it isn't quite as bright as it was last year. Go find your acrylic spray. (Hair spray will work very well also.) Spray your house all over with a fine mist. You'll be amazed at the revitalization of colors. If you've used the spray sparingly, your glitter should be just right. If you've used too much, dig out the old glitter and give the house a light dusting. There—ready for more oohs and ahs and spellbound children.

9.
Marketing Your Houses

*N*o matter what part of the country you live in, there seems to be a very lucrative market for selling gingerbread houses. Gingerbread houses symbolize the ideal holiday celebration, Grandma's house, and lots of presents and good cheer. Nostalgia opens a major market for gingerbread houses.

Before you rush out to sell your houses, however, check to see if there are any local laws and regulations to which you will have to adhere. I can't advise you as to the legality or nonlegality of selling gingerbread houses, but I strongly encourage you to research this area thoroughly before going into business. Your best source of information is your legal or financial advisor. He or she will be able to advise you of any licensing or registration requirements as well as the tax ramifications of selling your houses. But if you're determined to do this alone, contact the Small Business Administration in your area. This agency, funded by your hard-earned tax dollars, is the one part of the government I have found to be not only a most valuable resource but also a joy to work with. People there will hold your hand, talk you through any

business venture process, and assist you in your decision making, marketing, and bookkeeping. They'll direct you to the proper federal, state, county, or city agency for information on any licensing and insurance requirements in your area. So take advantage of them. You are, after all, paying for the services they provide.

Bearing in mind those serious bits of caution and the confidence that your gingerbread houses are far superior to those you've seen thrown together in various markets over the last few years, let's move on to the big questions.

How do I sell my houses without advertising? Well . . . To deliver a house I had made, I walked down main city streets to the man's place of business. In the four blocks I traveled, six people stopped to ask me where I'd gotten the gingerbread house. I just happened to have my card available to hand them.

I announced at a business meeting (twenty-five people in attendance) that I would be making gingerbread houses as gifts for the holiday season. I said if anyone wanted to order one, he or she should let me know by the end of the month (it was early October) as it took me some time to get a house together. Two of the twenty-five people ordered a house. However, on December 20, the group had a Christmas social, where door prizes (supplied by the members) were given to guests. I provided a small house as a door prize. Then another ten of the original twenty-five asked if I could possibly whip together a house for their mothers and/or mothers-in-law for Christmas. I gave them my GHF (Gingerbread House Fairy) card for the next year and then called them at the beginning of September. All ordered houses.

I took a gingerbread house to work to display in our reception area one year. Between the staff and customers who came into the building, I had more house orders than I could handle and had to train a friend to help.

The point I'm trying to make here is, *if people see the houses, you've got a sale!* So show your houses.

Businesspeople will want to order a house from you for a special gift for business associates or to decorate a Christmas party, or for the family, or all three. Take a sample house around to businesses in July . . . remember those real estate agents? One auto body shop owner ordered six houses one year, five for his top suppliers and one for his wife.

Some bakeries will agree to display a sample house with order blanks in exchange for a house they can use as a door prize in a drawing.

Some supermarkets (usually independents) will do the same. Offer them a house to use as a raffle prize for customers who sign up for a drawing. They can advertise the house drawing in their weeklies.

One owner of a small mall agreed to let me and a fellow gingerbreader set up a gingerbread house demonstration in the mall in exchange for a house he could use as a prize in a drawing. We prebaked and preassembled several houses, made the icing and sealed it into airtight containers, and brought all of our decorating equipment and set up two display tables in the mall. On one table we put decorated sample houses and order forms. On the other table we decorated the preassembled houses. The order forms included alternatives such as Christmas colors or pastel colors, illuminated or unlit houses, personalized or not. We asked for a 50 percent deposit on each house ordered and guaranteed delivery by a certain date. (December 1 is a very popular time.) We made a total of fifty-two houses that year and had to stop taking orders because there wasn't enough time to complete more. On top of it, we had a great time.

What do I charge for a house? When you are selling any-thing, you have to consider what it costs to produce. I calculate what each house costs me and triple this amount. For lighted houses, I charge somewhat more. If the house was a customized design, I charge considerably more. The range for gingerbread houses goes from less than $10.00 (the tiny ones with big candies and lots of icing on them) to $250 at an exclusive grocery market. One lady who took a gingerbread house class from me sold three houses at $75.00 apiece, the same style house this book helps you make. Again, figure what it costs you to make the house (don't forget to include your time) and add your time at a reasonable hourly rate. That will pretty much be your market value.

Here is a good example of how to price a gingerbread house. These calculations aren't set in stone, but are presented to give you a guideline. Though we had three different house designs, they were all essentially the same size, using similar amounts of cookie, icing, and candies. Figuring we spent about $15.00 on each house (base, gingerbread, icing, and candies) and it took us around four hours (we became *very* efficient) to bake, assemble, and decorate a house at $10.00 an hour, we sold our houses (unlit) for $55.00 apiece. We charged $5.00 more for an illuminated house. (We purchased the lights in bulk at $2.50 each.) Our order forms included options such as house style, Christmas or pastel colors at the base price ($55.00) with an additional charge for illumination. We negotiated separate prices for customized houses and indicated such on the order form. Delivery was included in the cost of the house (our choice so as to avoid having total strangers show up at our homes). As an additional note here, all the houses we sold were advertised as inedible—for decorative use only to avoid any conflict with local laws pertaining to the sale of food items.

How do I package my houses? When you deliver your houses to your customers, do it in style. Loosely wrap each house in colored cellophane and add a bow to the top (like a large fruit basket). On the cellophane wrap, pin or tie an envelope containing an instruction card explaining how to store the house; reiterate that it's not to be eaten (if this is the case); and offer to spark up the house and do general maintenance (if required) for a small fee in subsequent holiday seasons. You might also include your business card and/or an order form (make sure your name and telephone number are indicated) in case someone who sees the house while visiting your customer wants one too.

You also might want to provide a box in which the house can be stored. If you do, tape or use laminate sheets (available at any stationery store) detailing maintenance and storage instructions directly onto the box along with your name and telephone number. Don't forget to include the cost of the box in your overall price of the house.

Building a Portfolio

I take snapshots of all my houses, for several reasons. For one thing, that way I have a record of how I've decorated different houses and don't forget some great idea I used on a house I sold to old what's-his-name.

Second, I can indicate on the back of the snap to whom I sold the house. Then, when I go to do maintenance on it, I can arrive prepared with the right supplies. (Pretzels for fences seem to need the most repair—were they round pretzels or sticks?)

You also could indicate when you made the house. Then, after a few years, contact the customer to see if he or she'd like a new one.

This collection of snaps also makes a great portfolio with which to market your houses and is considerably lighter to carry around than houses. However, if your picture-taking talents are like mine, you're better off carrying the house!

10.
Conclusion

*W*e're at the end of this adventure in gingerbreading. After years of making houses, scanning magazines for more ideas, and gaining and losing multiple pounds due to eating, nibbling, and licking when I shouldn't have, I've never tired of making gingerbread houses. Perhaps it's witnessing the joy in a child's eyes when seeing a house for the first time, for even the smallest child recognizes the charm and fun of it all. Or maybe it's knowing that all of us can delight in naming the types of candy discovered on a gingerbread house, or wondering if a particular candy is still on the market because it certainly would have made a grand addition to this particular house. Never again will you have to wonder or worry about what to give someone for Christmas. Gingerbread houses always fit, I've never had one returned, and they're appropriate for people nine to ninety.

As I said in the beginning, gingerbreading is fun. It can be profitable. It is definitely satisfying when you're all done. Enjoy the house we've built together. Make many more in the years to come . . . for yourself, for others, for the fun of it.

Checklist for Building Your First House

Many of the items listed here you probably already have in your kitchen. The list is fairly comprehensive, so you won't find yourself in the middle of a process and discover, too late, that something is missing, or you've just done it backward and now have to practically stand on your head to complete it.

HAVE ON HAND OR PURCHASE

EQUIPMENT

__ an electric mixer

__ 2 cookie sheets

__ cooling rack (2 is better, 1 will do)

__ measuring cups and spoons

__ mixing spoon

__ sharp, straight-edged knife or X-acto knife

__ spatula

__ rolling pin

__ large (2 quart) pot

__ turntable (optional)

___ cloth kitchen towel

___ a couple of spice jars or small cans

___ small cookie cutters (optional)

___ food wrap (foil, plastic wrap, waxed paper)

___ brace for jelly roll sheets (optional)

___ glue gun (optional; for inedible house only)

___ large decorating bags

___ 6 standard-size couplers

___ metal decorating tips (sizes 16, 21, 3, 12 to start)

___ brush to clean decorating tips (optional)

___ Popsicle sticks (optional)

___ baseboard to set house on (at least 12 inches × 11 inches)

___ spool of rayon ribbon (optional)

___ light set and bulb (optional)

___ angel hair (optional; inedible houses only) or cotton

___ clear acrylic spray (optional; inedible houses only)

___ glitter, edible or not (optional; inedible kind for inedible houses only)

___ coarse sugar (optional)

___ emery board (optional)

___ square of felt or soft material (optional)

___ small tweezer (optional)

___ cellophane wrap (optional)

FOOD ITEMS

___ flour

___ vegetable shortening

___ granulated sugar

___ dark molasses

___ baking soda

___ salt

___ cinnamon

___ ginger (optional)

___ nutmeg (optional)

___ powdered sugar

___ eggs *or*

___ meringue powder

___ cream of tartar

___ food color paste (optional)

___ white corn syrup (optional)

___ candies (see list on page 49)

___ sugar ice cream cones (optional)

___ pretzels (round or matchstick size)

___ shredded wheat squares (optional)

___ graham crackers (optional)

Before You Begin, Decide

Is the house for eating or display only? If it will be eaten, use only edible products (no glue gun, angel hair, acrylic spray, or inedible glitter).

Is your house going to be illuminated or not? Prepare your baseboard for lighting before you assemble. Cut the windows and doors out of the dough before you bake.

Are the windows and doors to be cut out? Do the cut-outs before you bake the gingerbread pieces.

Will there be "glass" in the cut-out windows, or are they to be just open? If you put glass in your windows, glue it over the inside of the windows before you assemble the house.

Will window glass be made of cellophane or candy? You must make candy glass before you assemble the house.

Does the house need to be braced? Brace your house before you assemble it.

What yard accessories will you want? Assemble and/or decorate trees, bushes, lampposts, and so on before you start to decorate the house so the icing can dry.

Will you be decorating the inside of your house? Decorate the inside before you put on the roof.

Sequence of Steps

1. Prepare the pattern (pp. 8–9).

2. Prepare the baseboard (p. 19).

3. Bake the cookies (p. 26).

4. Make the icing (pp. 31–32).

5. Assemble the house* (p. 35).

---

* If you're going to decorate the inside of the house, leave the roof off.

† You can put the roof on before you decorate the outside of the house, or after—whichever is easier for you.

6. Decorate the inside (optional) (p. 41).

7. Put the roof on and decorate it† (p. 41).

8. Decorate the outside (p. 47).

9. Put icicles on the house (p. 88).

10. Put decorations in the yard as you snow it (p. 82).

11. Snow the yard and add the fence (p. 86).

12. Glitter the house with edible glitter while you snow it *or* spray and glitter the house *after* letting all the icing dry hard (four to six hours) (p. 91).

13. Trim the baseboard with ribbon (p. 94).

14. Settle back and enjoy everyone's reaction!